HUMANIZING JEWISH LIFE

BOOKS BY DOV PERETZ ELKINS

Worlds Lost and Found (With Azriel Eisenberg)
Treasures From the Dust (With Azriel Eisenberg)
Olamot She-Ne-Elmu Ve-Niglu (Hebrew translation of
    Worlds Lost and Found), Tel Aviv
*So Young To Be a Rabbi: The Education of an American
    Clergyman*
*Rejoice with Jerusalem: Prayers, Readings & Hymns for
    Israel Observances*
*A Tradition Reborn - Sermons and Essays on Liberal
    Judaism*
God's Warriors: Dramatic Adventures of Rabbis in Uniform
*Shepherd of Jerusalem - A Biography of Rabbi Abraham
    Isaac Kook*
Humanizing Jewish Life
Glad to Be Me - Building Self-Esteem in Yourself and Others
Clarifying Jewish Values
Self-Esteem Group Training
Self-Concept Sourcebook

HUMANIZING JEWISH LIFE

Dov Peretz Elkins

SOUTH BRUNSWICK AND NEW YORK:
A. S. BARNES AND COMPANY
LONDON: THOMAS YOSELOFF LTD

©1976 by A. S. Barnes and Co., Inc.

A. S. Barnes and Co., Inc.
Cranbury, New Jersey 08512

Thomas Yoseloff Ltd
Magdalen House
136-148 Tooley Street
London SE1 2TT, England

Library of Congress Cataloging in Publication Data
Elkins, Dov Peretz.
Humanizing Jewish life.
Bibliography: p
Includes index.
1. Jewish way of life. 2. Fellowship (Judaism)
3. Temple Beth El, Rochester, N.Y. 4. Elkins,
Dov Peretz. I. Title.
BM 723.E5   296   75-38456
ISBN 0-498-01912-8

ON THE COVER

The plate on the cover comes from Persia and was probably a kind of amulet or protection in the home; it may have been hung on a wall.

The 67th Psalm, woven through the branches of the menorah, was often used to guard the household. It begin: "God be gracious unto us and bless us . . ."

Above the menorah are the Ten Commandments, flanked by the Lions of Judah, symbolic guardians of the faith. The Twelve Tribes of Israel gird the upper rim of the plate. Above them is the saying: "God, Guardian of Israel (Psalm 121:4)." Below them, on the right and left, are two sayings found in Deuteronomy: "This is the Torah that Moses placed before the Children of Israel." and "Moses commanded us to keep the Torah. It is a goodly inheritance for the Congregation of Jacob" (Deut. 4:44; 33:4). The Sh'ma appears on the lower right rim and praises to God (Psalm 71:8) appear on the lower left.

The colors, especially the brilliant blue, are characteristic of Persian art. The Stars of David, encircling the Islamic symbol of the crescent, are typical of Judaica from the Near East.

Two mysteries remain. The date of the plate is one—experts we consulted placed it in a three hundred year range, somewhere within the 17th, 18th or 19th centuries. The second mystery is the writing on the base of the menorah, the platform for the two larger lions. Our experts agree the text is not Hebrew. However, some say it is Aramaic; some say it is Persian transliterated in Hebrew; some say it is coded Hebrew gematria.

The Persian plate comes from the collection of Fern and Ronald Kaplan, Brookline, Mass. The above explanation and the photograph are reprinted by permission from MOMENT, The New Magazine for America's Jews, founded by Leonard Fein and Elie Wiesel. Volume 1, No. 2, July/August, 1975.

PRINTED IN THE UNITED STATES OF AMERICA

Dedicated to my teachers and friends
in the field of human development:

Edward Thornton
James Ashbrook
Sidney B. Simon
Howard Kirchenbaum
Merrill Harmin
Carl Struever
Bob and Dot Bolton
John E. Jones
Tony Reilly
Jack Canfield
Judy Ohlbaum-Canfield
Eric Rennert
Paul McVey
Elaine R. Elkins
Jerry and Elisabeth Jud
John O. Stevens
Will Schutz
Jan Rugh
Margaret Sawin
Luz Baytag
Jim Robinson
Robin Reid
Bill Pfeiffer
Tony Banet
Jack Gibb
Lyman Coleman
Bernie Schwartz

Contents

Introduction

Since this book is a collection of articles, speeches and activities, it needs an introduction to unify its various threads.

At first I thought of sitting down and writing a book, from cover to cover, about some ideas I have on humanizing synagogues and other Jewish organizations and communities. But that would take a year of nothing but thinking, reading and writing, which I don't have right now. Then, I realized that an even better way would be to gather together my own personal experiences in humanizing Jewish life. They would be more real, more concrete, and more practical. So that is what I did.

One of the most exciting books I ever read in my life was Carl Rogers' *On Becoming a Person,* which is a collection of Rogers' articles, speeches, and essays. Together, the papers in Rogers' book present a tapestry of his life and thought. I am hopeful enough to think that the principle operating in that case might also be operating here—namely, that all the articles and talks in this book will present a nice picture of my image of a synagogue and of Jewish life and education as it should be.

The approach in this book is *humanistic.* Contrary to what the uninitiated reader might think, that does not mean ethical culture, God-less religion, or anything of the kind. It means, simply put, *person-centered.* I believe, passionately and completely, that Jewish life—as I understand it—must become more person-centered. I believe that that's what the Bible is and that's what the ancient teachers and sages wanted Jewish life to be—*humanistic,* or person-centered. In the words of my late teacher, Abraham Joshua Heschel, the Bible is not a book about God, but rather it is a book about man.

Some Jews think synagogues, religious schools, Jewish organizations, Jewish communities, should be Israel-centered, or Hebrew-centered, or tradition-centered, or ritual-centered, or ethics-centered, or synagogue-centered, or rabbi-centered, or building-centered, or fund-raising-centered. I believe that these are all incomplete and that the only holistically authentic Jewish institution and community life is *person-centered.*

Arthur Combs explains in the best way, through a concrete example, what person-centered is and means in education. One can apply the idea to all of Jewish life, including synagogues, religious schools, Federations, and community centers:

In one of the schools in the outskirts of Atlanta a very lovely girl was teaching first grade. This young woman had beautiful long hair which she was accustomed to wearing in a pony tail down to the middle of her back. She wore her hair this way the first three days of the school year. Then, on Thursday, she decided to do it differently. She did it up in a bun on top of her head, and went to teach her first grade. Well, one of her little boys came, looked in her room, and did not recognize his teacher. That sometimes happens when a woman changes her hairdo. So the little boy was lost, all by himself out in the hall.

Soon, along came a supervisor who said, "What's the trouble?" He said, "I can't find my teacher." The supervisor then asked "What's your teacher's name?" Well, he did not know, so she said, "What room are you in?" but he did not know that either. He had looked in there and it was not the right place. So she said, "Well, come on. Let's see if we can find her," and they started down the hall together, the little boy and the supervisor, hand in hand. She opened the doors of several rooms without much luck. Finally, they came to the room where this young woman was teaching. As they opened the door the young teacher turned, saw the supervisor with the little boy standing in the doorway and said, "Why, Joey, it's so good to see you, son. We were wondering where you were. Do come in. We've missed you so." The little boy pulled out of the supervisor's hand and threw himself into the teacher's arms. She gave him a hug, a pat on the fanny, and he trotted to his seat.

While the supervisor was telling me this story, she and I were riding along in a car. She said to me, "Art, I said a prayer for that teacher, she knew what was important!" We got to kicking this around; suppose she had not thought little boys were important, suppose she thought supervisors were important? In that case she would have said, "Why, good morning, Miss K., we've been hoping you would come and see us, haven't we, boys and girls?" And the little boy would have been ignored. Or she might have thought that the lesson was important. In that case she would have said, "Well, Joey, for heaven's sake, where have you been? Come in here and get to work." Or she might have thought that the discipline was important. In that case she would have said, "Joey, you know very well when you are late you must go to the office and get a permit. Now run right down there and get it." But she didn't. She behaved in terms of what she believed was important, and so it is for each of us.

Abridged from "The Human Aspect of Administration" by Arthur W. Combs in *Educational Leadership* 28(2): 197-205; November 1970.

One last word. This book is designed to be more than a collection of psychological and educational theories. There are more than enough books on that subject already. Its strength,

I believe, is that it contains practical, concrete, specific ideas, progams and activities for rabbis, teachers, community leaders, social workers and group facilitators to utilize in their own process of humanizing Jewish life.

Humanizing Jewish Life is the fruit of my own experience at Temple Beth El, Rochester, New York. I cannot complete this introduction without thanking all the scores of marvellous people in that wonderful congregation who were part of the experiments described here. They made it all possible.

My wife, Elaine, deserves special thanks for encouraging me to take risks, to do strange things, to experiment, and to be brave enough to walk where fools fear to tread. She has been an active partner in all of the work I have done in humanistic psychology and education in my congregation.

I am very grateful to my devoted secretary, Pearl Ostroff, for her constant help in all things, and for typing these pages. I am also grateful to Mona Friedman for reading the proofs and compiling the index.

It is my fervent prayer that some of the new and different paths described in this book will help spread the revolutionary ideas of the humanistic, person-centered, approach which I espouse, to other synagogues, schools, Jewish organizations, and communities throughout the world.

HUMANIZING
JEWISH LIFE

Man is not yet human. He is only a candidate for humanity.

Mordecai M. Kaplan

Man cannot approach the divine by reaching beyond the human; he can approach Him through becoming human. To become human is what he, this individual man, has been created for.

The true hallowing of a man is the hallowing of the human in him. Therefore, the Biblical command, "Holy men shall you be unto me" has received Hasidic interpretation, "Humanly holy shall you be unto me."

Martin Buber

Each Jew knows how thoroughly ordinary he is; yet taken together, we seem caught up in things great and inexplicable. It is almost as if we were not acting but were being acted through . . . . In Deuteronomy, we are told that even then we were "the smallest of people." How many are we? The number of Jews in the world is smaller than a small statistical error in the Chinese census. Yet, we remain bigger than our numbers. Big things seem to happen around and to us.

Milton Himmelfarb

The Searcher

I looked for my soul
But my soul I could not see
I looked for my God
But my God eluded me
I looked for a friend
And there I found all three.

William Blake

PART I
Humanizing the Synagogue

1
The Synagogue as a Growth Center

The synagogue, as it exists today, has been, in many ways, a failure. I think one of the reasons, perhaps the main reason for the failure, is because we are looking upon the synagogue in the wrong way. I don't mean to imply that this is merely a semantic problem. When I say looking at the synagogue in the wrong way I mean those who conceive of the synagogue, who direct the synagogue—the staff, clergy, teachers—as well as those who direct it from a lay point of view—officers, national, regional, local lay leadership.

The old model of the synagogue is a model of an institution of religion. I don't think a synagogue should be an institution of religion, mostly because few people today are really interested in religion. Then, too, most people are not interested in tradition-bound institutions. Thus, the combination of institutionalism and religion is a totally losing one. The synagogue is supposed to foster Jewish identity, to teach religion and to prevent assimilation and intermarriage. It hasn't done any of these things very well. I don't think it can.

I think if we look upon the synagogue in a new way perhaps we can recreate and revitalize it into a different kind

Unedited transcript of a talk delivered to Jewish Community Federation, Rochester, N.Y.

of force in American Jewish life. I won't call it an institution. I don't know if there is another word, not in the old model, certainly.

The model I would like to suggest is that of a growth center. I don't know if that word is familiar. It is a new concept in American life.

A growth center is simply a place where people go to grow spiritually, emotionally, and intellectually, a place where people go to become better human beings. It's a very simple formula, and yet the simplicity of the formula dwarfs the fantastic potential of the concept that lies beneath it.

If we begin to see everything that happens within the four walls of the synagogue and outside of its walls, under its auspices, as opportunities for human beings to fulfill their potential, to become fully functioning, happy, healthy, fulfilled people, to find meaning, purpose, and commitment in our lives, then the synagogue might begin to succeed. Much of what I am talking about comes out of the new sciences of humanistic psychology and humanistic education.

Abraham Maslow, a great human being and a great Jew, the late professor at Brandeis University, revolutionized modern thinking, as far as I am concerned, in terms of how we look at people and how we look at life. He began to look at human beings differently than anyone ever did before. He was a psychologist and was interested in psychotherapy and the study of human behavior and experience. He did it in a radically different way. He didn't look at sick people to find out how people should be well. He looked at well, happy, constructive, and fully functioning people. Nobody ever did that before. It is an amazing thing. He found that fully functioning, creative people have certain characteristics. He listed about fifteen of them, boldness, wholeness, aliveness, uniqueness, their interests in justice, simplicity, playfulness, self-sufficiency, among them.

It seems that if we looked at things that go on in the synagogue in these ways—how they bring about these qualities within the participants—I think we would be doing everything differently and much more efficiently. Learning programs which take place now on the adult and youth level, formal and informal (meaning our religious schools, our youth program, our adult institutes), would be done not just to transmit language, or even the content of books, but to transmit these books, ideas, theories, and concepts that have come to us from the past, in terms of how they *affect our lives* and how they can help us to search for values which will enable us to survive meaningfully in today's society.

There is a whole new world now in education. We don't utilize these new approaches in our religious schools (any more than most of our public schools do), so we are failing. Our adult institutes and every educational level that we pursue today are failing because we have the wrong kind of model.

I think our worship experience has to be looked upon as an experience of potential growth for human beings. A search for and an expression of ideals, a binding of ourselves in an over-arching unity with the universe, with the world, with God, searching out for a transcendent peak experience. That's not what we do. We look upon worship as fulfilling the mitzva of reciting the words in the prayer book because the Schulchan Arukh says we have to recite those words. We have to *daven* three times a day. We have to say this prayer or that prayer. We have to say it this way and that way. We are so concerned about the details of doing it in the way tradition says that we forget the over-arching purpose of it all which should envision the synagogue as a place where a human being should grow and become fully functioning. Then, prayer will become a different thing because we will see some use for modern prayers and for interpreting the old prayers and in making the service meaningful, not just rote recitation.

One of the important ways that people grow and fulfill themselves is by finding joy and satisfaction in life, by finding fulfillment in the daily rounds, weekly Sabbath, special occasions and holy days, and milestones in our personal lives. For example, birth, coming of age, bar/bat mitzvah, bris, naming a baby, wedding, funeral, marriage—all of these rites are opportunities for celebration, opportunities for recognizing the important stages of human life. As we reach each milestone, we have to look at and ask ourselves how far have we come as human beings? These, then, become opportunities for celebrating life, for joining together as a community for the purpose of recognizing the important milestones and highlights of human life and existence.

The Sabbath would become an opportunity to surpass the technological dehumanizing urban society in which we find ourselves instead of a mere fulfillment of the commandment, "Thou shall keep the Sabbath." That is important only insofar as we see it as an opportunity for human betterment. If the synagogue is a place for human growth, then it can function as a successful institution.

Everybody wants to become a better person, but not everybody wants to become religious. The word "religious" has Christian connotations. When Judaism became a religion it began to go downhill. It never was a religion. Judaism was a way of life, a way of life to teach you to become a better person. We forgot that when we came to the western world. Therefore, everything became institutionalized under the rubric of "institutionalized religion." What I am saying is that we have to get away from these Christian notions and get back to the old Jewish notions of the Torah as a guide to life, not as an opportunity to become "religious." "Religion" doesn't appeal to me. Too many Reform, Conservative and Orthodox Jews look upon religion as some kind of a box that they have to fit themselves into. That's not my conception of what Judaism is all about.

I see the synagogue as a growth center or, more precisely, a center for the growth of Jewish human beings. I think that this new model can radically transform what goes on in synagogues.

Everything that goes on in the synagogue has to answer certain questions. Examine each activity. (I don't like the word activity so let's call it happening. Activity implies business for the sake of business.) Each event in the synagogue should be analyzed by using the following criteria: 1.) Are people being helped to achieve their full human potential? 2.) Is the focus on *individual,* and not on rules, laws, customs and institutions? The old model is stultifying and sometimes dehumanizing. Are we helping people to become more mature, more fulfilled, more purposeful in their lives? Are we helping them to relate better to one another as human beings? When you walk out of a worship service, do you know how to relate to someone better than you did when you went in? Have you discovered more deeply who you are? What are your values? If you haven't, then you went through the motions and wasted your time.

Looking at the synagogue in this way changes everything, including worship, ritual, education, sermons and the image of the leaders of the synagogue (both professional and lay). The roles of the rabbi, the educator, the teacher, and the hazzan change. They now become people who facilitate the human growth of their charges, their flock, where they had seemed to be people who lay out rules and regulations and make demands, give out orders and do all the other things that most clergy people do in America. They become people who facilitate the growth of other human beings.

A brief word is in order on what I mean by growth. I mean very definitely religious growth which includes psychological growth but is more comprehensive. I am not conceiving of the synagogue as a therapeutic out-patient clinic. Not at all. I am talking about religious fulfillment at its highest potential. That to me is what everything in Judaism is all about. I have studied the Torah, the Talmud, the midrash, the siddur, medieval poetry, and philosophy. Everything I have studied in Judaism has little to do with what we in America consider to be "religion," an institution, or the synagogue. It has to do with how people become better human beings. I think that creating a new image of the synagogue in the 20th century will help us do what traditional Judaism really set out to do many centuries ago. That goal is the creation of purposeful, self-actualizing, self-transcending human beings within a community that fosters values of truth, justice, peace, hope, love, and fulfillment.

2
Family Life Council

In September 1973, Temple Beth El of Rochester established a Family Life Council. A Family Life Council is a new concept in synagogue programming, unique, to my knowledge, in the American synagogue.* It can best be described in terms of its structure, goals, and programs.

STRUCTURE

The Family Life Council is a Temple committee, like a school board or youth commission. In function and structure it is co-equal with other committees, such as a house committee or an office practice committee.

The membership of the Council is mostly couples, rather than individuals—highlighting the specialized objectives of the Council. To foster one of the goals of the Council, the Family Life Council encourages couples and families to be together when planning as well as attending Temple activities.

*The idea for a Family Life Council came from Rabbi Sidney Greenberg of Philadelphia. The scope and particular activities and program of our Family Life Council, however, are much different.
This essay was published in the *Reconstructionist,* September, 1975.

GOALS

1. To sponsor activities for *entire family units* within the congregation—or part of family units, such as married couples. Many Temple activities and programs are geared primarily for individual members of the family, such as school, adult education, youth program, men's club, and sisterhood. It is the task of this Council to sponsor activities for the entire family.

2. To encourage other temple arms (Men's Club, Sisterhood, Adult Education Committee) to sponsor total family activities.

3. To sponsor educational activities to teach such themes as marriage enrichment, human sexuality, communication, self-esteem, and parenthood. Such courses fall under the rubric of "Jewish Family Life Education."

4. To help individual members and families develop a sense of micro-community within the larger temple community. These micro-communities will help integrate members into the temple family and act as safe, nurturing family-like groups in which individual growth and development of religious and moral values takes place.

5. To foster a sense of warmth, trust, openness, and mutual support within the temple community and to create a sense of "Chevrusah" or "religious community" within a large institutionalized religious congregation.

6. To design and sponsor innovative programs for fostering achievements in Jewish education, community observances, experiencing of Shabbat and festivals, creative and meaningful prayer experiences within the context of tradition—all for family growth. Such programs include retreats for adults, youth, or whole families, value clarification activities, and other programs in humanistic (person-centered) education.

PROGRAMS

THE HAVURAH

The Havurah Program began in September, 1973, simultaneous with the inception of the Family Life Council.

We now have 15 Havurot of approximately twenty people each. The Havurot consist of single and married adults meeting monthly in homes of members. Some Havurot consist of a single age group, while others cover many age groups. Some 300 people are involved in this program.

Requests for information about our Havurah programs have come to our temple from some fifty different Conservative congregations.

THE MISHPACHA

The Mispacha Program began in January, 1974. Unlike the Havurot, the Mishpacha, or substitute extended family (also called "Family Cluster" and "Second-Chance Family"), is made up of entire family units, including children of all ages, and adults of different generations. Also, unlike the Havurot, it is not leaderless, but has a trained facilitator who prepares meeting designs for each session and carefully evaluates each session following its completion. My wife and I were the facilitators of the first Mishpacha group along with a paid consultant in Christian religious education from a neighboring Unitarian Church. Other Mishpacha facilitators received in-service lessons and other workshop professional training in group process, educational design, and Family Cluster facilitation.

JEWISH FAMILY LIFE EDUCATION

Courses, lectures, and sermons on issues and values in Jewish Family Life Educaton are also part of the responsibility of the Family Life Council.

Some courses are designed and sponsored by the Family Life Council in conjunction with the Rochester Jewish Family Service, and other programs, lectures, and sermons are sponsored by other temple arms and given advice and support assistance by the Family Life Council. Some of the special courses held were:

1. Parent-Teenage Dialog on Human Sexuality (4 Sessions), Spring 1974
2. Child-Rearing (8 sessions), Fall 1973
3. Making a Good Marriage Better (6 sessions), Fall 1974
4. Parent Effectiveness Training (8 sessions), Fall 1975
5. Stages in the Life Cycle (5 lectures), Nov-Dec 1973

RETREATS (KALLOT)

Youth Retreats:

Youth retreats helping to foster a close sense of community and utilizing content material in Jewish family life education have been held in October, 1972, October, 1973, October, 1974, and June, 1975. A grant of $4800 was received from a Rochester charitable foundation for three experimental youth retreats based on principles of Jewish humanistic education and values clarification. Designs for these retreats are created by me in conjunction with consultants from the National Humanistic Education Center in Upper Jay, New York.

Adult Retreats:

An experimental, innovative adult retreat, with a theme of "Building Self-Esteem", was a special supplement to Jewish Family Life Education. It was held in March, 1975, and was an overwhelming success. Approximately 25 adults participated. It was held in a motel in a nearby community. Other retreats (Kallot) are now being planned for the 5736 program year. The first adult retreat was designed by myself to integrate principles learned from humanistic psychology, humanistic education, Jewish existential theology, group dynamics, and adult Jewish education.

EVALUATION

All of the programs sponsored by the Beth El Family Life Council have been well received and widely acclaimed by participants. Many have attracted national attention. A description of others is now in preparation for national dissemination.

The congregation has felt the effects of all of these programs in many different ways, including increased involvement by individual members and families in temple activities; strengthening of Jewish family life and personal and family development; fostering of an atmosphere of warmth and a sense of religious community at religious services and other public temple functions; and increased opportunities for adult and youth Jewish education through the modalities of small groups meeting in informal settings.

The Temple's Board of Trustees has given much praise and endorsement to the participants in the Family Life Council for their innovativeness, creativity, involvement of peripheral as well as active temple members, and imaginative religious, cultural and educational programming.

It is our hope and plan to expand our present program offerings and continue to innovate new programs, drawing upon resources and ideas within the Jewish and general community as well as deriving assistance from the modern social sciences towards fostering human and educational growth and development.

FAMILY LIFE COUNCIL PROGRAMS

PROGRAMS IMPLEMENTED AT BETH EL, ROCHESTER

1. Havurah (15 groups of approximately twenty people each)
2. Mishpacha (two groups existing, two more being formed; approximately 25 people in each group, intergenerational)
3. Jewish Family Life Education (Human sexuality, marriage enrichment, parent effectiveness, life cycle)
4. Kallah (retreats held at motel, camp, retreat center, over Shabbat, with study and experiential components)
5. Shabbat dinners for entire Temple

OTHER POSSIBLE PROGRAMS FOR FAMILY LIFE COUNCIL ON DRAWING BOARD

1. Care for the Aged in the Congregation (Driving to Temple events, services, visits to Old Age Home, etc.).
2. Congregational Second Seder, with everyone taking parts.
3. Foster Grandparent program matching older and younger families on individual basis.
4. Congregational picnic.
5. Hospital and Nursing Home Visitation.
6. Para-professional lay counseling.
7. Mitzvah Committee - to call families of people in hospital and ask if help needed, and render services where needed.
8. Seudah Shlishit for entire congregation.
9. Tu Beshvat Family Outing, Tree Planting Ceremony.
10. Assist in Sukkah Building for entire congregation.

HAVURAH ACTIVITIES

1. Shabbat and Festival dinners.
2. Guest Speakers.
3. Attendance together at adult lecture, Selichot services.

4. Break-the-fast meal together after Yom Kippur.
5. Israeli Folk Dancing at Purim Time.
6. Visit Russian Jews who recently moved to Rochester.
7. Evening with the Rabbi.
8. Joint Havurah meeting - youngest Havurah with oldest Havurah to dialog about synagogue.
9. Pesach Seder.
10. Building a Joint Sukkah.
11. Catering Bar/Bat Mitzvah for a member.
12. Prepare meal after return from cemetery for member who suffered death in family.

FAMILY LIFE EDUCATION COURSES

1. Child-rearing the No-lose Way
2. Marriage enrichment - Making a Good Marriage Better
3. Parent-Teenage Dialog on Human Sexuality
4. Communication Skills
5. Self-Esteem for Individuals and Families
6. How to Be More Assertive in Life
7. The Jewish Family - Where to Now?
8. The Life Cycle

MISHPACHA ACTIVITIES

1. Each person brings an object from home - something special that says something about himself/herself. Members sit in a circle, and each shows what he/she brought and explains why it is important to him/her.
2. "Person Tags." Instead of "name tags" for the first meeting, each person took a 5" x 8" index card and wrote his name, one thing he/she likes to do, and one thing he/she hates to do. Members mill around room and non-verbally read each other's *person tag.*
3. Either/Or Game. Participants were asked to stand at one side of room if they chose alternative A, and the opposite side if they chose alternative B. No "compulsive moderates" were allowed to stand in the middle. This activity forces value choices. Sample alternatives: city-country; morning-evening; giver-receiver; vanilla-chocolate; spender-saver; organized-chaotic; follower-leader; Jew-American.

4. "You Can't Make a Turtle Come Out." Group learned this catchy song, and discussed its implications. No one can be forced to participate in any activity (or in anything in life) unless willing. (Reference: *Little Boxes and Other Handmade Songs* by Malvina Reynolds; Oak Publications, 1964).

5. Writing of new, current versions of the "Ha-Rachaman" section of Birkat HaMazon.

6. "Listening Walk." Group goes outside on a nice day and walks around area with trees, bushes, non-verbally—just listening to sounds and viewing sights. Walk is done in teams of one child and one adult, not of same family. Return and share impressions.

7. In preparation for a Mishpacha Shabbat dinner, each person listed things he knew and didn't know about Shabbat. People read what they didn't know, and if someone had that information on his list of "did know" he shared it. Otherwise leader helped.

8. Shabbat dinner, with each family bringing special kiddush cup from home and explaining its importance. Some members baked challah.

9. Family Coat of Arms. Each family made its own "Coat of Arms" from cutting out pictures and words in old magazines, posterboard and construction paper. Families were able to search for what is important to them. Some of the themes were: Share and Care; Do Things Together; Promote Good Health; Support Israel; Retire Energetically. Each family explained its Coat of Arms.

10. Tu Beshvat Celebration. Each person brought in a poem, story, object, dealing with trees. Each family brought fruit to share with whole group.

11. Writing, preparing and acting of a brief skit before residents of Jewish Old Age Home.

12. Visit to Chabad House in Buffalo for full Shabbat.

3
Education by Families - A New Learning Model

About three years ago, I began pursuing studies toward a doctorate in pastoral psychology and family life education at Colgate Rochester Divinity School. A guest speaker in the course on family counseling was the Reverend Dr. Margaret Sawin, education minister at the First Baptist Church in Rochester. Dr. Sawin pioneered in the field of creating substitute extended families through which she was able to create meaningful experiential learning. Dr. Sawin now conducts workshops throughout the United States for facilitators of what has now become known as the "Family Cluster."

Our congregation decided to experiment with a similar program, adapting it to our own Jewish style and taste. Instead of "Family Cluster" we called our group "Mishpacha." The Mispacha is similar in many ways to the Havurah program initiated by Rabbi Harold Schulweis, but includes children as a fundamental and integral part of the experience. This gives an entirely different flavor to the group, and changes the format in significant ways. (Beth El of Rochester also has fifteen Havurah groups operating and a few participants in Mishpacha also belong to a Havurah.)

Published in the *United Synagogue Review,* Spring, 1976.

We now have two Mishpacha groups and hope to start one or two more in the next few months. Since I feel that this program is the most significant achievement we have created in the last several years at Temple Beth El in Rochester, I am anxious to share a description of how it works and some of its great successes.

The need for a new model of Jewish education grows out of several problems. First is the fact that traditional Jewish education has failed so often that any innovation with promise of success should be carefully examined for possible uses. Secondly, the new burdens the modern family must bear are vastly more weighty than those a family was called upon to carry in years past.

In a recent article in *The Family Life Coordinator,* a family expert writes: "The mark of our time is the peculiar disharmony of the individual's relations with the wider society. There is a trend toward a sense of lostness, aloneness, confusion of personal identity. One effect of this trend toward disorientation is to throw each person back upon his family group for restoration of a sense of security, belongingness, dignity and worth. This pressure to compensate individual members with special security and affection imposes upon the family an extra psychic load."

In my view, the purpose of the synagogue is to foster individual growth. The means through which this goal is achieved include prayer, ritual, education, and creating a sense of community. Since the family is one of the most effective vehicles to achieve human growth, the synagogue should work through its structure to achieve its goals. Education about life (through Jewish sources) and about family communication should find a natural base in the synagogue environment.

The first Beth El Mishpacha group (Mishpacha I) began in January 1974. My wife and I met with our Temple's Family

Life Council and persuaded them of the importance of trying to establish a Family Cluster at Beth El. Once the idea was accepted we engaged a consultant in the person of the education director from a Unitarian Church across the street which had already done work in the Family Cluster program.

We announced the availability of the Mishpacha program to the congregation and received a good response. Eight family units were selected from among the respondents (a family unit can consist of a single person or a family with several children). The two main criteria for selection were: a) that there would be more than one child in each age category in order to provide adequate peer companionship, and b) that there be a wide range of ages represented, including grandparent figures, to assure a chronologically representative substitute extended family.

In most cases, the families with young children did not have grandparents, aunts, uncles, and cousins in Rochester, and the grandparents in the Mishpacha did not have their own children and grandchildren living in the city. We each filled a gap missing in the lives of other group members. If the experiment would work, we would fill a great emotional and psychic as well as religious need for our members. Events centering around the holidays and life cycle milestones would now be enjoyed by our entire Mishpacha together, and we would reduce the incidence of loneliness, isolation, and the "sense of lostness."

Each prospective family in the Mishpacha was interviewed by my wife and myself, with our consultant, to explain the purpose and goals of the experiment, and to receive from them a firm commitment to attend all meetings unless emergency circumstances arose. The initial contract was for ten meetings, one a week, on Sunday evenings from 5 to 7:30. We began the first week in February, 1973, and concluded in mid-April.

At an average meeting, the first fifteen minutes are concerned with straggle-in activities, which prepare for the evening in some way. These activities include creating a name-tag for oneself. On it are any identifying characteristics, like favorite sports, books, seasons, abilities, and even some fears that one might have. During the next half-hour, the group engages in a pleasurable, recreational game, such as checkers, chess, art work, or team-building activities. This might be something as silly-sounding as "chuckle-belly," in which one person lies on the floor, the next person following with his head on the belly of the preceding, until all 28 members are lined up like a train, each his head on the belly of the preceding. Then, the first person yells out "Ha" in the form of a laugh. The second person says it twice, and the third person three times. By the time the fourth or fifth person takes his turn guffawing, the entire community of 28 are roaring in hysterical laughter.

After forty-five minutes, we would open our brown bag dinners (milchig) and enjoy a fellowship meal, replete with motzee, birkat hamazon, and Israeli singing, all family style. At 6:30, we would engage in some learning experience, such as writing new sections of the birkat hamazon, telling stories about a coming holiday, making a collage about what our family life means to us, or discussing the latest events in the Middle East. Having children from age four to grandparents in their seventies all engage in this family educational experience, each on his own level, was one of the priceless values of the Mishpacha experiment.

Unfortunately, we live in a "split-level" society which is marked by age segregation. Our children's values are most often gained from their peers rather than from their parents and other adults. The intergenerational learning environment of the Mishpacha helped overcome this unfortunate phenomenon. In Jewish life, the family has always been the garden for the growth of values and religious attitudes.

The last fifteen minutes would be taken up by the Family Council, a meeting of the entire Mishpacha, discussing what happened that day, making plans for coming meetings, airing unexpressed feelings, and creating some closure for the day. In this experience, too, children and adults have an equal voice. Finally, the friendship circle, with the singing of Shalom Haverim.

In the words of Dr. Sawin, creator of the Family Cluster model, "Learning derived from the experiences one has in the family is probably the most lasting and impressionable of a person's lifetime." For this reason, we find that the Jewish education that takes place, both formally and informally, at Mishpacha gatherings, can be far more influential than that which occurs in the classroom of the Religious School, which so often has turned off young people to meaningful Judaism. Perhaps more positive living experiences in Ramah, USY, LTF, and in Mishpacha will help motivate children enough to want to derive greater benefits from their formal classroom experiences. The Mishpacha is in no way designed to replace standard religious education, but it can supplement both the content and motivational level of classroom education.

Mishpacha I decided to continue meeting after the initial ten week contract on a once-a-month basis. We have now been meeting regularly for eighteen months and continue to grow closer together. Family tragedies have been shared, simchas celebrated together, and some wonderful learning experiences have taken place. Mishpacha II began in January 1975 and decided after its successful ten-week commitment to meet twice a month. It is co-facilitated by three adults who participated in Mishpacha I, and who attended several workshops for advanced training in Family Cluster leadership.

Many meaningful educational, religious, and social experiences have grown out of Mishpacha. Several Shabbat dinners have been held for which members bake their own Hallot. Mishpacha II recently returned from a camping weekend, during which Shabbat, Judaism, the beauty of nature, and learning to relate effectively were combined in a moving weekend experience. A Bat Matzvah was catered from A to Z by one Mishpacha which gave enormous emotional as well as material support to a family that was emotionally drained trying to get through a difficult experience which they would not have been able to handle alone.

It is becoming increasingly apparent in our congregation that this innovative model has tremendous potential for Jewish education, for strengthening Jewish family life, and for overcoming much of the alienation and anonymity of modern life. As the number of people in the world increases, there seems to be less and less meaningful contact between whole persons. In a highly mobile, computerized society, the Mishpacha is an effective learning model for intergenerational communication, extending emotional support, experiential education, and significant gains in family life skills such as communication, decision-making, conflict resolution and others.

Congregations interested in experimenting with the Mishpacha model are invited to write me for further materials and suggestions at 100 Palmerston Road, Rochester, New York 14618.

APPLICATION FOR MISHPACHA

Mishpacha is a family-oriented program designed to bring people into a substitute extended family experience. It includes the entire family with **equal** participation for all of its members. It involves an initial commitment of ten consecutive weekly meetings.

NAME _____ Marital Status:

      First   Last

                                           Married _____

Spouse's Name (if applicable) _____ Widowed_____

                                           Single _____

Address: _____

                                Zip

Phone_____

Age Range: Under 30____30-40____40-50____50-60____Over 60 __

Children: Names   Sex   Age

_____

_____

Family interest and hobbies: _____

_____

_____

Reasons for joining a Mishpacha: _____

_____

_____

Please return to: Mishpacha, Family Life Council, Temple Beth El, 139 S. Winton Road, Rochester, New York 14610

4
Our Family Cluster

by Elaine Elkins

PROJECT

The purpose of my project was to introduce into our synagogue program a Family Cluster Program, to form the first cluster, and to co-lead it. This was all to be done in conjunction with my husband who is the rabbi of the synagogue.

WHY THE SYNAGOGUE?

Mental Health deals with the wholeness and fulfillment of people and their relationship to self and others. Churches and synagogues must be involved in the Mental Health revolution in order to be relevant to contemporary human needs. If churches and religious leaders do not involve themselves in Mental Health and meet the emotional and value needs of their congregants they will find themselves without congregants in the near future.

My wife, Elaine Elkins, was instrumental in planning and facilitating the first Mishpacha at Beth El. Her co-facilitation of the Family Cluster was credited as field work for a course in group leadership which she took in partial fulfillment of the requirements for her master's degree in counseling. This paper is her description of the project that she submitted to her professor.

OBJECTIVES

1. To provide extended family experience and support for those people who need it. The old extended three generation family is disappearing. Increasing mobility means that for a great number of Americans, relatives live long distances away. Technology and urbanization have changed work patterns so children are often not even in close contact with their fathers. The Family Cluster is an attempt to create a substitute extended family and to increase the interaction between parent and child to help create a supporting web of human relations.
2. To provide a small and intimate group for discussion and celebration for members of a large congregation. (We have 1300 families.)
3. To present and explore healthier ways for families to interact. The Cluster will be a human laboratory for better communication and interaction among members of the families involved.

STEPS

1. To convince the Board of Trustees and the Family Life Council of the synagogue of the validity of the project and get permission to introduce it into the synagogue program.
2. To introduce the idea to the congregation at large and to get enough volunteers to form at least one Family Cluster. We will interview all volunteers and pick out about six family units for our first Cluster.
3. To set up the pilot Cluster and co-lead it with my husband and Jan Rugh, Director of Religious Education at the Unitarian Church who has had much experience in leading Family Clusters.

We arrived in Rochester a year and a half ago, when my husband took over the pulpit of Temple Beth El. It became clear to us that if this synagogue was to be a vital and thriving religious institution and fulfill the needs of its members, the program as we found it would have to be enlarged. We found that the lay leaders, sensing the need for these changes, had looked for, found, and expressed delight in having a rabbi committed to creativity and dynamic change.

My husband and I became familiar with the Family Cluster Program through a friendship with Richard Gilbert, minister of the neighboring Unitarian Church and our meeting with Margaret Sawin, teaching minister of the First Baptist Church in Rochester. Both of them lead Family Cluster Programs in their churches. This past fall we became convinced of the value of and need for introducing this program into our synagogue. We read two publications on the Cluster program. One was called "Developing an Extended Family," printed by the Unitarian Church in Santa Barbara, California. The other is a loose-leaf put together by Richard Gilbert as a "guide prepared to introduce you to the Family Cluster concept of religious education and to help you in implementing Family Clusters in your church."

We knew we would have a difficult task in getting approval for the Cluster program from the Board of Trustees. Because the concept is new and because some of the activities in which the cluster members participate are unfamiliar (such as sensitivity work), they are threatening, misunderstood, and judged as being far-out or radical. My husband was, however, able to convince the Board to form a new synagogue committee called the Family Life Council. The purpose of this Council is to plan *all kinds* of projects and activities for family units. This committee was perceived as a creative, non-threatening suggestion by the Board and won approval. When the Family Life Council members were appointed we made sure that more than half were young, open-minded, receptive people.

In October, we held the first meeting of the Council at our home. We discussed the purposes of the Council, the needs to be met in the synagogue, and various programming possibilities. We then introduced Ms. Jan Rugh, Educational

Director of the Unitarian Church, who described the Cluster program in her church. She spoke about Clusters, and then presented a slide show that began by illustrating the impersonalization of life and how people are segregated by class, race, age, and are often isolated and alone. Then, a number of slides of Clusters in action were shown. These slides showed people of all ages, all kinds of family units—singles, young, old, children together sharing, eating, talking, worshipping, having a good time. Jan explained the Cluster as a way to create a substitute extended family, improve family communication, clarify family and personal values, and gain insight into oneself. It is a place, she said, where all have the right to be heard. It is a means of achieving intimacy within the framework of a large, often impersonal institution.

As expected, many people were very excited and enthused by her presentation. Some were turned off and upset. Some couldn't begin to understand the need for such a program. They stated that they felt no void in their lives. There are, in fact, hundreds of people in the congregation who feel alienated and isolated and who are looking for meaningful experiences in the synagogue. Others could recognize the existence of the needs but couldn't accept the synagogue as the place for satisfying these needs. Others were turned off by the slide scenes in which people were touching or adults were playing. It took much time and patience to deal with these objections. I played an active role in this discussion and was able to help many people understand the reasons for the cluster. I was also a facilitator in helping many people understand and cope with their anxieties about the kinds of things we would be doing. At the end of the discussion we put it to a vote and it was decided that we would organize one pilot Family Cluster for a ten week period. Based on the outcome of this cluster, we would decide whether to expand into a larger program. Going through this decision process was a meaningful experience. It made me very sensitive to the fears people have about changing things or trying new things. Most important I learned how afraid people are to learn to know and love themselves or others around them. I could see how upset people were when they saw slides of people touching or of adults playing together on the floor. It upset people to see slides of people looking at each other and talking about things they care about. It told me a lot about myself that these slides did not upset me. Instead, I relish the opportunity to have such experiences. It also helped me to understand that as a leader in such a situation one must deal patiently but persuasively with others to create trust and to help them to accept and not be afraid.

We were pleased at this point that we had the permission to proceed. We engaged Ms Rugh as a professional advisor. Her role would be to train us in two areas, one of which was organization—how to select people, how to interview people, and how to set up the cluster. The other area of instruction was in leading the cluster (the kinds of activities, ways to put people at ease, etc.). Of the ten consecutive meetings, Ms Rugh attended the first five and helped lead them. After that, we were on our own.

The next step was to introduce the cluster idea to the congregation at large. This was done through a series of sermons on two Jewish holidays when all congregants were sure to be in synagogue. Two sermons dealt with the problems of modern day society (mobility, alienation of people, indifference, insensitivity, loneliness, impersonalization). The third sermon dealt with what the synagogue could do to help resolve some of these problems. The idea of the Family Cluster was presented as one possible way. The sermons were received enthusiastically by many and negatively by a few.

We then sent a mailing out to the congregation asking for registration in the Cluster program. We met with Jan Rugh and she offered many helpful guidelines for selection of families: to make sure there are all ages in the group, to match children up making sure there are at least two in each age group, to avoid having people in the same profession (they'll shop-talk), to have more children than adults, to avoid immature families, etc. Bearing these suggestions and others in mind we selected seven family units (including our own). We picked two couples over sixty whose children are grown and away from home, one couple in their forties with three children, three couples in their thirties with three children each, one couple in their thirties with one child, and one single woman in her late twenties.

The next step was the interview process. The interview was not really a means of selection but a way of confirming our choices. In the interviews we were able to meet the families, find out their expectations, and tell them our expectations. In effect, we laid out the ground rules. If our expectations and theirs were similar we proceeded. If, in the course of the interview, it became clear that they could not make all the commitments necessary, that they misunderstood the purposes of the Cluster, or that there were any serious family or marital problems, these families were eliminated from the group at this point.

INTERVIEWS

There were a number of things Jan Rugh advised us to stress during the interviews. First, families should be asked to make a serious ten week commitment and be prepared not to withdraw or be absent unless absolutely necessary. Second, the cluster is a place for talking and for *all* to have the right to be heard including children. Children are to be considered full participants. Third, this is not to be considered a therapy group. Fourth, group members should be ready to approach new people and new kinds of activities with an open mind and a good amount of tolerance—to give everything and everyone a chance. And last, to stress that we appreciate the anxieties that people have and that we will try to make our experiences non-threatening. We want our times together to be relaxed with time for inter-change and sharing over meals, songs, talking, and play.

To date, we have interviewed six of the families during a period of two weeks. We have found the people excited but nervous and apprehensive. This is to be expected. All the families interviewed proved suitable candidates. They were all enthusiastic and prepared to make the commitments we required. In the interview process we tried to relax them, to talk about their apprehensions, and to help them feel less anxious. They all expressed the fear of being pushed too quickly into relationships with strangers. We assured them that there would be no pressure and that we would take our time getting to know each other. Some of the families with small children expressed doubts about their children's behavior and/or ability to participate. We stressed that all children would be encouraged to participate to the extent that they could and to the extent that they were willing. Any child would be free to leave the structured activity at any time to go off to play if he desired. Ms Rugh told us that children normally flow in and out of the group especially during a structured activity and she suggested we provide a play area with toys for them.

The above are the characteristics that were typical of most of the families. Each family interviewed, however, had a unique quality about it.

5
Mishpacha

"The large synagogue is dying." "The day of the cathedral congregation is at its end." So we hear. But I am not certain. Synagogues still need large budgets and large school enrollments and large memberships to have adequate staff specialists in administration, music, education, and other areas. We still need a large enough constituency to provide significant turnouts for major programs in which we invest time, talent, and energy.

Given the existence of the large synagogue and all the impersonal nature which it often reflects, what ways are there to bring home the message of Judaism to the individual member or member family? A novel idea, proposed and fostered by Jacob Neusner, is the Havurah. The Havurah is a small group committed to Jewish study, Jewish living, to relating to one another in community. Its purposes, goals, programs, and several examples of implementation attempts, are all carefully explained in Dr. Neusner's book, *Contemporary Judiac Fellowship* (Ktav), which I strongly recommend.

Today, however, Christian churches are carrying the Havurah idea one step further, *mutatis mutandis.* Many of

This article appeared in *Beineinu,* Journal of the Rabbinical Assembly, January 1974.

them are establishing family havurot, which they call Family Cluster Groups. A Family Cluster is a surrogate extended family. Given our mobile society, many families lack the privileges, blessings, and joys of having grandparents, aunts and uncles, cousins, and other relatives within visiting distance. We are alone, on our own, unattached to the meaningful associations that make life easier, more meaningful, and more love-filled. What do we do?

Can the church/synagogue supply a substitute for this extended family of olden days? Can an older couple join with a younger family, and adopt each other? Can a bachelor male become an uncle to a father and his children, who no longer have a mother? Can families with young children and families with teenagers join and become "cousins": Can such emotional ties be forged in this artificial way without the benefit of blood relationships? Can there be a small group of five or six such families, old and young, with some children, some whose children are grown and living elsewhere, some without partners, all joined together to become a surrogate extended family group (Family Cluster, Family Havurah, or Mishpacha) for six months, or a year, or, hopefully, much longer?

This is the experiment. Basically, in most cases, a group is chosen and meets together for ten consecutive weeks. Some may want to continue. Others will drop out. Some friendships, and loving relationships, may develop which are permanent. Who knows? The experiment is too new to gauge or evaluate its effectiveness. But is has great promise and it is spreading around the country.

Following are some resources for developing such "Family Havurot":

1. Dr. Daniel I. Malamud, a psychologist, has a long booklet of discussion and research which he will share with readers for a fee of one

dollar for costs of duplication and shipping. Write to: Dr. Daniel I. Malamud, 49 E. 96th Street, New York, New York 10028.

2. Dr. John A. Crane, a Unitarian Minister, has done extensive experimentation in the Family Cluster field. He has prepared a booklet which has already been distributed in the hundreds around the country to fellow clergy. He, too, would like one dollar (make checks to "Unitarian Church") for the booklet:

> Dr. John A. Crane
> Unitarian Church
> 1535 Santa Barbara Street
> Santa Barbara, Calif. 93101

3. In my community, a dynamic and creative female minister with a doctorate in education has been training family cluster leaders and lecturing on her successes. Dr. Margaret Sawin has compiled three booklets describing her creative experiments in religious education. One is called "The Learning Community," and goes for $2.50. "The School of Religion" sells for $1.25. Finally, "Family Clusters" is also $1.25. All three, bound together, come for $4.50 (add 7% sales tax for New York State residents). Write to:

> L.E.A.D.
> P.O. Box 311
> Pittsford, New York 14534

Start with reading Jacob Neusner's book, *Contemporary Judaic Fellowship,* and then the above. See, also, my review of *Joy,* by William Schutz, in the Winter, 1972 issue of *Torch,* and the other books listed there on small groups in the church/synagogue.

The following books will also be of help: *Spiritual Renewal Through Personal Groups,* John L. Casteel, Association Press, 1957.

The Creative Role of Interpersonal Groups in the Church Today, John L. Casteel, Association Press, 1968.

Groups Alive-Church Alive, Clyde Reid, Harper & Row, 1969.

Sharing Groups in the Church, Robert C. Leslie, Abingdon Press (paperback), 1970.

GUIDELINES FOR HAVURAH PARTICIPANTS

1. Activities must be conducted in the framework of Shabbat, festival, and Kashrut observance. Host families who do not keep kosher can usually serve milchig refreshments, dinner, etc., provided this is okay with group members. No one's religious convictions should be violated by the group. Temple standards should also be kept.

2. Be patient and tolerant. Compare your group to a "family." Surely you do not feel as strongly about every cousin, aunt, uncle, or even sibling, as you do about others. We all have preferences, and yet we learn to respect, and often feel affection for those who differ from us, disagree with us, and have qualities which sometimes annoy us. Do not expect every member of your group to be perfectly matched in every way. After sharing experiences, especially a great *simchah* (a Bar Mitzvah or wedding) with Havurah, or a deep tragedy (a death or a crisis), you will feel more strongly for each other despite any personality differences. Be patient and tolerant! In June, changes can be made in some reshuffling of members. Until then, try to get to like your havurah-mates. Remember that they have the same problems you do in accepting others, and the same privileges.

3. Try to be open, warm, and accepting. Risk yourself. Trust more than you usually do. Remember that the people in your group need you as much as you need them. In this crazy world, we all need to huddle together. That's the purpose of Havurah.

4. Be imaginative and creative. You have ideas you never thought of. Don't be afraid to try something new. Be open-minded about new ideas, about accepting other's attitudes.

5. You know yourself best, what qualities you should stress in relating, and which ones you should improve. Shy people should make an extra effort to participate. Extroverts should try to help others become more involved, and be careful not to monopolize. There are no spectators in a Havurah, only participants.

6. For resources, feel free to call upon the Temple staff for speakers and discussion leaders. For problems in the Havurot, call the Rabbi.

7. As much as possible, let there be a Jewish theme at each meeting—a discussion, a report, a film, a holiday dinner, a celebration, a party. Part of the purpose of the Havurah is to try to become better Jews together.

8. The Rabbi would like to know what issues you want him to discuss in his sermons. When a problem issue arises, it might make a

good sermon. Let him know, and the Havurah can attend, listen, and then discuss it at the next meeting.

9. Remember, this is not an encounter group or therapy group! Don't analyze your neighbor, or think you can solve his/her problems. Share feelings, *your* feelings, but not your opinion of his/her emotional problems or hang-ups. Be careful in passing judgment or in identifying neurotic behavior patterns. It is fair to tell a person that you are angry, that's expressing *your* feelings. It is not fair to try to help him by suggesting that he act differently. That's for him to decide, and not for you to impose. In group dialogue, express *your* *feelings* rather than stressing *others'* actions.

6

What Is a Havurah?

What is a Havurah? This seems an appropriate question as we come close to the end of the 5735 season and begin to plan for the Temple's fall program. Our congregation now has 16 Havurot, or fellowship groups. They meet monthly, in homes of members, or at the Temple, or sometimes at a theatre, a lecture, or other special place or event. Some are comprised of couples and individuals who are contemporaries, and some include individuals of all ages, from twenty on up. We have received requests from rabbis, educators, and interested lay persons from all over the country to tell them about our Havurah program.

The Havurah program was launched during Yom Kippur services almost two years ago, when I devoted my Kol Nidre and Yom Kippur morning sermons to the concept of the Havurah. Since two years have now passed, perhaps it is time to review our goals and objectives.

Our Temple is a large one. With 1300 families, we number over 4000 souls. In such a large institution, it is difficult to get to know people well. It is often difficult to feel comfortable at Shabbat and holiday services, and other educational, cultural and social activities at Temple. When an indi-

From the Temple Bulletin, May, 1975.

vidual has a close relationship with 15 or 20 others, it is easier to feel comfortable in a crowd, and to feel at home and at ease. Our Havurot have achieved this goal beautifully. Members of Havurot tell me frequently that they attend services and other Temple activities much more often now with the members of their Havurah. The Havurah will make a date to attend the Beth El Discussion Group on a Saturday night together, to attend the Temple Hanukkah dinner, or Purim party, or Sisterhood Dance, or whatever. This gives me great pleasure, since that means that one of our major goals is being achieved: the integration of our members into Temple activities in a meaningful and enjoyable way.

A Second goal for our Havurot is the enrichment of our personal lives with friends who share our interests, objectives, and cultural heritage. The Havurah is not meant to be just a social club, even though it does provide opportunities for relaxed social enjoyment. The meetings of the Havurot by and large are discussions, lectures, attendance at a cultural event, a religious observance such as a Passover Seder, as well as picnics, parties and other outings.

What distinguishes the Havurah from other more socially-oriented clubs is that its members share an interest in Judaism, Jewish intellectual stimulation, Jewish observance, Jewish education, and Temple Beth El. Not all of their activities are culturally or religiously oriented, but many are. Even when socializing, Havurah members know that their last activity, or a coming activity, will focus on some Jewish experience. This provides the glue and the substance (excuse the mixed metaphor) of the Havurah. This is why our Havurot have been meeting for two years now and most are still going strong. Groups which are entirely socially directed often fall apart after a short while for lack of purpose and direction.

We live in a highly mobile society and the Jewish population of our community, like other Jewish communities throughout the country, is becoming increasingly transient. When new members join the Temple, we immediately offer them an opportunity to join a Havurah and find a meaningful way to integrate themselves into the Temple and Rochester Jewry. Having pulled up deep roots from another community, Jewish individuals and families are able, through the Havurah program, to overcome the sense of loneliness, isolation, and alienation that would otherwise beset them.

There are two more goals of the Havurah program. First, to help members enjoy and celebrate special Jewish occasions, such as Shabbat, festivals, and personal and family milestones. Some of the Havurot have enjoyed an Oneg Shabbat together, a Friday night dinner, a festival service, a Sukkah party, a post-Yom Kippur break-the-fast meal, and like activities. Today, many of us have our parents and grandparents, children and grandchildren, living in other cities. The Havurah can thus serve as a substitute extended family.

When personal simchas and tragedies arise, such as Brit, baby naming, Bar or Bat Mitzvah, wedding, and even illness or death, Havurah members during the past two years have been there to help. When death robs us of loved ones, Havurah members have helped with arrangements, baby-sat for children, prepared refreshments for visitors, and other chores which would normally be done by members of the family. For native Rochesterians who have their own family in town, the friendship, warmth, and sharing of joy and tragedy has meant a great deal even when physical arrangements are already taken care of.

The fourth and last goal—but by no means least—is the opportunity for adult and family Jewish education. Much Jewish learning takes place in the Havurah meetings, both formally (lectures, discussions) and informally (visits to Chabad House in Buffalo, Pesach Seders). Our members become more knowledgeable and more observant Jews through their participation in Havurah.

To review, then, our Havurot have achieved the following things:

1. Integration of Temple members into congregational activities
2. Enriching our lives with meaningful friendships among people who share common goals and help each other overcome the loneliness and isolation of modern society
3. Celebration of Shabbat, festivals, and personal and family milestones
4. Opportunities for formal and informal Jewish education

Why not join a Havurah this Spring, in time for the coming year of 5736?

7
Havurah and Mishpacha - Transcript of Discussion

Transcription of two discussions on the Havurah and Mishpacha Programs at the home of Rabbi Dov Peretz Elkins, Wednesday evening, June 11, 1975

Temple Beth El's Family Life Council came into existence in October, 1973, to promote activities within the temple which would strengthen Jewish family life.

The Family Life Council sponsors such diverse activities as Family Life Education, Kallot (retreats), Shabbat group activities, Havurot, and Mishpacha.

Below is the transcript of two discussions which took place on Wednesday evening, June 11, 1975, at the home of Rabbi Elkins. The first discussion is concerned with the Havurah Program. Beth El has fifteen Havurot and has had one of the most successful Havurah programs in the United States (second only, in quantity, to that of Valley Beth Shalom, where Rabbi Harold Schulweis founded the Havurah Program). Some 300 people are involved actively in Havurot.

Participating in the discussion of goals, achievements, and future concerns of the Havurot are Rabbi Dov Peretz Elkins, Phyllis Kasdin, and seven congregants who have been chairpersons (coordinators, facilitators) of their own Havurot, Sam and Dorothy Shoolman, Iris Saltzburg, Stuart and Sandy Stern, Annette Eisenstein.

Each Havurah has approximately ten couples and in some cases one or two single adults. They meet monthly, mostly without their children, in homes of the members, and sometimes in other settings, such as the Temple.

The transcript of the discussion follows:

This is Rabbi Dov Peretz Elkins of Temple Beth El, Rochester, New York. We have assembled here tonight seven members of our Havurah program, all of whom have served, at one time or another, as coordinators of their own Havurah. The Havurah program has been in existence for about two years now. We have roughly fifteen groups going of approximately ten couples each. We want to discuss tonight some of the various aspects of the Havurah program. First we ought to start with the goals. How do you see what the Havurah program is created for, why was it created, what things should we be doing in the Havurah program? Who would like to start?

Sam Shoolman: De-institutionalize the Temple. Beth El has over 1300 families and my experience in over a third of a century with Beth El is that people no longer participate. They are members, come Rosh Hashana and Yom Kippur. The Havurah group enables them to meet with 10, 12, 20 people, meet them on Shabbat and feel as if they are part of Beth El.

Iris Saltzburg: Along the same lines—even people who attend Shabbat services regularly. Come on a Shabbat morning and there are at least 400 or 500 people there. It is very difficult to make any kind of a close relationship. But the Havurah groups give you an opportunity to know well 10 or 15 or 20 people whom you then see and feel quite at home with during a service. It's a place for a newcomer to begin.

Rabbi Elkins: When somebody joins the congregation they can immediately have an "in" or a slot to fit into and don't feel they are part of the big mass of people with no base of operations.

Dorothy Shoolman: It also serves a function for people who have been life-long residents of Rochester, whose families are no longer around or are looking for other avenues. They have met new people and they are seeing faces that they have never seen before and can't believe that these people perhaps have been members of the congregation as long as they have because their paths have never crossed. This has served another need for them.

Rabbi Elkins: Do you think we should look at the Havurah program as a vehicle for Jewish education? Is that asking too much or is it a realistic goal for this to be a vehicle for Jewish learning and knowledge?

Phyllis Kasdin: I think we have proven the fact that the groups that have a study purpose are more cohesive and survive in a better way. Some groups decided to be truly social but after a few social meetings discovered that this wasn't enough to hold them together. So they have evolved a study purpose so I think it is a marvelous form of adult education.

Rabbi Elkins: Should the Temple structure the program or leave it to the groups?

Phyllis Kasdin: It varies. I can't really say. I think some of the groups now are beginning to realize that they need a study purpose and some of them are starting to get a particular theme going for next year. Some of them sort of studied in a haphazard way. At one meeting, they would have one person come and talk to them about a particular topic, at another, somebody else. Five of the groups got together to hear Rabbi Gurary, the hasidic rabbi. It isn't all purely social. Even the things that are social are learning experiences. They are people in the groups who have never celebrated the holidays, who have had seders together and this is a learning experience. The Havurah groups have built sukkot together and this is a learning experience. They have done things which they have never done on an individual basis but through their groups they are now doing it. So it is an educational experience even when they get together to have fun.

Rabbi Elkins: There seems to be a big emphasis on holiday celebrations.

Phyllis Kasdin: Right. That's part of it, too. Some of the groups have done more than others because each group is very unique and each group has taken on its own particular complexion. You can't really say any one thing about the whole program because each group is very different.

Rabbi Elkins: I think we ought to say something about the program of these groups. We really haven't given them any specific directions, left each one on his own and let them follow the way which they think is appropriate for themselves. Has this been too permissive? Has it created any difficult circumstances for the groups to flourish? Would it have been better for us to lay out the programs, the format, and say here's what to do, do it our way and you will succeed?

Speaker: The regular meetings of the coordinators were very helpful. Ideas were adopted from one group to another. I don't think the group would have lasted without that much help.

Iris Saltzburg: I put another interpretation to your question of guidance for the groups. I thought you meant that we should say, "all right, everybody must study, everybody must do this and so." I would disagree with that strongly. As Phyllis has said, many of the groups have found that just socializing isn't

enough. They must have some other function. I can speak for
the group to which I belong. In its first year, we had a general
interest in hasidism around which our meetings revolved more
or less formally throughout the year. The second year of its
existence we decided not to do anything like that, but kind of
let things flow as they would and whoever was the host would
provide some sort of program. The group continued to meet.
We are all very happy to see each other but most often we just
sat around and chatted. We decided that that really did not
work for us and we have now selected a topic for our third
year. In celebration of the bicentennial we are doing Jewish
history in America.

Rabbi Elkins: You found out for yourselves that study was
what you wanted. If the Temple had said you had to study,
you probably wouldn't have come to the conclusion with the
willingness as you did this way.

Iris Saltzburg: Absolutely. We found that it was right for our
group. I would still not be willing to say that it is right for
every group.

Stuart Stern: As the coordinator of the young adult groups we
found that we do need some leadership. If my wife and I had
not acted as coordinators, we found that different people have
not really come across and done the job we have asked of
them. So we have acted as leaders. We have set up a program
of dual aspect. We have a social aspect and a religious aspect.
I think, from my own personal feelings, I have certainly done
a lot of things in Jewish life that I probably would not have
accomplished. I led a seder and I know that my parents and
my wife were quite surprised, to put it mildly, about how well
it came off. We have had interesting discussions learning
about kashrut. We had a very deep discussion about the
holocaust. We broke the Yom Kippur fast together and these
things have all taken on a different and a better meaning to

me, and I think, to the whole group. We have had someone besides our family—most of our group is from out of town and don't have a great deal of family in the Rochester area—and here they have been able to come together, celebrate a holiday together and feel a part of something, feel they are Jewish and want to show their Jewishness and enjoy the holidays the way they are supposed to be celebrated.

Rabbi Elkins: What I am hearing most of you say is that the goals of the Havurah were more or less achieved, in one way or another. Are there any goals which were not achieved, or any goals which were achieved with a special emphasis?

Sam Shoolman: I think that now that these groups have been going for two years there should be more coordination in leadership. I think there are some groups that are not finding themselves and do need suggestions. I don't mean that someone should instruct them in what to do, but I think suggestions ought to be made as to fields of education and speakers. I find there has been a lot of duplication and I find that some of these people just don't know who to call and what arrangements be made. I think in the future there should be more coordination between the groups and there is need for more professional guidance.

Rabbi Elkins: There have been coordinators' meetings every three or four months. Have these been helpful to give these kind of ideas, programs and structures?

Stuart Stern: I think we have gotten out of hand at some of these meetings because there are too many people. A meeting is fine but the meeting we want to try to conduct in just two hours, we get hung up on one subject—I can't think of any in particular—but I know that an hour and a half of a two hour meeting is wasted, hanging up on one subject. Maybe we need more of a central coordination committee that are the main coordinators of the whole body but every three or four months we should have a big meeting for all the coordinators of the different groups and we can pass ideas out through them and find out any of the problems that are going on. Hopefully, not get hung up the way I feel we did in the past.

Rabbi Elkins: Let's take a few minutes to go over some of the highlights of your particular havurot and your programs, things that happened during the meetings, between the meetings, or some of the programs. What stands out in your minds during the past two years of really meaningful experiences in the Havurot or with members of the Havurah?

D. Shoolman: First, I don't think the people in our group would have ever come together in other situations had it not been for the Havurah. We learned from them and from each other. Our group is mixed and the older age group and we all had different backgrounds. They had a lot to offer to us and we shared a lot of things that we otherwise would not have.

Iris Saltzburg: My group is a heterogenous age group ranging from a couple in their twenties through to a lady in her middle seventies. The vast majority are in our forties and fifties, I would say, which may color the group considerably. However, we have been able to share the preparations for the wedding of the young couple that are in our group, some of the difficulties of our older members. We have been able to share a Passover seder which was extremely meaningful to all of us. We have mourned the death of a child of one member together and, in many ways, have acted to each other as surrogate familes.

Annette Eisenstein: Ours is the same type of group—from a couple in their twenties to a woman close to 70. In this case, a woman who is single, never been married and she has found it a meaningful experience. She has enjoyed it tremendously and can't get over how wonderfully she blends with the rest of us. And with the youngest couples we celebrated and shared with them the experience of their first child, the naming of the child. There is another member of our group who would really frown terribly on any organized religion and yet this is the one group he joyfully comes to and even to Temple to name this new baby who is like the grandchild he perhaps will have himself. So it has become an extended family and we have shared a good number of the holidays together and perhaps some of us are the older sisters and brothers to the younger ones, others are the grandparents, or the parents that we don't see, and the grandparents of the younger children, where their grandchildren are out of town. It's been a very warm experience. When my daughter can say this is like the cousins I don't have, that's a great feeling.

Rabbi Elkins: I hear a lot of people talking about children. Actually the Havurah program was not designed specifically for including the children. That was the Mishpacha. But I see that despite us, many of the groups do include their children and it is a very interesting phenomenon. I really wasn't aware of the extent and degree to which there is this total family involvement. It is not continuous and ongoing, but even occasionally the kids feel that they know the children of the other families and really appreciate it.

Annette Eisenstein: They know the adults as well and feel very free and comfortable in speaking to them on the phone. My son had an experience for USY just recently and had no qualms about asking an adult to help out (a member of our Havurah). He was only too glad to do it.

Rabbi Elkins: Any other highlights, things which stand out in your mind?

Sam Shoolman: The highlight in our group culminated in a meeting where Rabbi Gurary talked about hasidism. I think most of the fifty or sixty people who were there were surprised to know that there is such a movement. They knew nothing of the Habad House. There is a part of Judaism which most people have forgotten about. I think another highlight of our group is their interest in Beth El. The number of people who felt they wanted to participate in its activity and indicate that this type of group could be a powerful force for change especially with women's liberation and women's participation. I think there is a real ferment and if Beth El's policy will change, these groups will be very strong in helping bring about the change.

Stuart Stern: I think one of the true highlights of our group, the young couples group, in their late twenties, maybe early thirties, was during our first year when we met twice, on different occasions, with the young rabbinical student who came in from New York to spend weekends at Beth El. He seemed to provide a great deal of depth for our group and everyone felt that this was a truly rewarding experience and something that we could relate to. This is one of the true highlights of our first two years.

Speaker: Having the opportunity to meet with the Rabbi and the Cantor, having them visit our group, was a highlight.

Dorothy Shoolman: The young group, those in their twenties, requested a meeting with those of us in our sixties to learn of our experience with Temple Beth El. What the Temple offered to us, what benefits we had had, what advantages they might look for. That was a very good meeting.

Rabbi Elkins: What do you think we ought to do from now on? What's the direction for the Havurah program, or the groups? Are there any pieces that are missing? Are there any new programs that have to be initiated? Let's talk about the future a little bit. Anybody have any ideas?

Phyllis Kasdin: It's my hope that every member of the congregation will become a member of a Havurah. We want to get everybody interested and there is a lot more interest because it has been extremely successful and people are hearing about the success of the program and want to get on the band wagon. We have 1300 families so it is going to take a bit of doing to get everybody involved in the program. Over 300 people are now involved in the Havurah program. An interesting thing is evolving. I think we will see more of it and that is single people wanting to join and not necessarily wanting to be in groups with other single people. They want to be in groups where they can be accepted as an individual, not necessarily as a couple, and I think this has happened in the Havurah. Everybody is accepted as an individual and many people who are widows are joining Havurah, looking for relationships, and finding very meaningful relationships within the groups. They do not feel uncomfortable being in a group where most of the other people are couples. Right now most of them are couples but there are single people and more single people are becoming interested and I think this will open up a tremendous avenue and fulfill a tremendous need in our congregation for the single people.

Rabbi Elkins: Anyone else want to take a look down the pike—three to five years—where we should be going, where we might be heading, what the Havurah can be doing for Temple Beth El. Let's suppose we had a Temple filled with forty or fifty Havurot. What effect would that have? I think, just as an aside, our congregation probably has the most successful Havurah program in the country with the possible exception of Beth Sholom in Encino, Calif. where Rabbi Shulweis is, the founder of this whole program. I think next to them, we are the most successful with our fifteen very successful groups. Suppose we had forty or fifty groups and everybody was a member. What might that be able to do for our Temple? Would it change the complexion of our Temple?

Phyllis Kasdin: I think it would make it a warmer place. Many people walk in—it's a large, awesome, beautiful building—when you walk in you are immediately faced with many, many strangers. Even though you will not personally know that many more people than you know now, at least there will be those members of your group, 25 people perhaps, that you do feel very comfortable with and will give you a warmer feeling when you come into Temple, overcome this feeling of coldness that newcomers feel. And even people who have been members for many years, because the complexion of the congregation changes, even they have felt, "I don't know anybody any more." But they will have their Havurah group and therefore will feel a certain warmth when they come into Temple.

Stuart Stern: I think there is going to be more of a willingness for people to participate in Temple activities. I found during the Temple year when there were functions going on, I normally don't think that my wife and I would go to a Friday night dinner by ourselves because we probably wouldn't know the people very well. Now, with our Havurah group, we call a few couples and say, let's go. Not "do you want to go?" They are always willing to go. Sunday mornings, we participate with the Men's Club, too, but we go as a goup. Sometime you are reluctant to go as an individual but this way you have a group. As a new couple or person joins Temple, they should be made fully aware of what the possibilities are. Certainly for a young couple from out of town, the best opportunity in the world for them to start to know the Jewish population in Rochester, to get to meet different people, express different ideas, learn, become friendly, and want to stay with Beth El and possibly stay in Rochester is through the Havurah.

Iris Saltzburg: I would agree with all of these goals save one point. I am not sure that Havurah is for every member in the congregation. Not every one who joined originally decided to stay with it, for many different reasons. It is not the kind of thing that everybody should be expected to participate in. A person who joins a Havurah must be able to accept other people as they are, must not demand that everyone they meet with be like them and agree with them on everything.

Rabbi Elkins: People who join a Havurah could learn, adopt a new attitude, to accept people, wouldn't the Havurah then be achieving more and really act as a humanizing agent?

Iris Saltzburg: Absolutely. Don't misunderstand me. I'm not saying that anyone should be excluded from Havurah. I am saying that it should not be expected that everyone will want to be part of it. It could be beneficial to them if they wish to make that effort, but they must be willing to make that effort and not everybody is.

Dorothy Shoolman: I think no more than twelve to fifteen couples, tops, would be an ideal group to have.

Iris Saltzburg: I don't think Rabbi was suggesting that the individual havurot become larger but rather that there be more of them.

Dorothy Shoolman: I think the tendency might be to make the group larger. Several people wanted to join ours and we had to limit and ask them to be a part of other groups because of physical limitations.

Rabbi Elkins: What has been our success in getting new Temple members to join a Havurah? We have fifty to seventy-five new families every year. Has it been useful to them?

Phyllis Kasdin: Yes, I think about half the new members who join the congregation joined the Havurah this year. When the prospective member meets with the Membership Committee, they are told about the Havurah program at that time and are given an application. We started to call all the new members who had not joined and everyone we spoke to was well aware of the program and each had a different, very valid reason why they couldn't join at that particular time, but perhaps in the future. I think half is a very good percentage!

Rabbi Elkins: I think we have had a very good overview of the Havurah program. Phyllis, can you tell us something about some of the programs in which all of the Havurot joined together?

Phyllis Kasdin: We had two programs for all the Havurah groups. The first one was held last August—a square dance in the Temple and about 150 people attended. It was extremely successful. Everybody had a marvelous time. All the groups worked on it. Everybody took on a different job. It was a lot of fun. It gave everybody a chance to meet with everybody else in the Havurah program. The second party was a Purim party and it was an evening of Israeli dancing. It, too, was a lot of fun. People got together to meet other people in the Havurah program and, through these two programs, members of the Havurah groups feel a certain affinity towards other members who are in different groups because they are sharing the same type of experiences through the program. We plan on having more of these over-all Havurah groups in the future.

Rabbi Elkins: Being a member of Beth El and a Havurah brings them into closer contact with other Beth El members and makes the whole congregation feel more like a small intimate community.

That's a good place to conclude. Thanks to everybody for participating. Shalom!

MISHPACHA DISCUSSION

Below is a transcription of the discussion on the Mishpacha program. It differs considerably from the Havurah Program. It is made up of five family groupings, including some families with children, grandparent figures, single adults and children of all ages. About twenty-five to twenty-eight people are included.

The Mishpacha program is a venture in inter-generational experiential education. It has been described as a "Family Cluster" or substitute extended family. Many of the people in the Mishpacha have parents and grandparents in other cities. Likewise, the older participants often have their children and grandchildren in other cities. The emotional, physical and spiritual support of the old-time extended family for most people no longer exists. The Mishpacha is designed to fill that serious gap in American family and community life.

Each family is interviewed by two trained co-facilitators prior to the start of the group. They must commit themselves to ten consecutive Sundays from 5 to 8 p.m. The group meets in an informal room at the Temple and brings their own dairy dinner. The experiences of these three-hour programs are designed carefully in advance by the facilitator (unlike the Havurot whose programs are often planned by the entire group for the group).

Facilitators of Mishpacha I (January-March, 1974) were Rabbi Dov Peretz and Elaine Elkins, and a paid consultant from a local church, one of the originators of the "Family Cluster" program in the Rochester area, Ms. Jan Rugh. Mishpacha II (January-April, 1975) was co-facilitated by three people who were members of Mishpacha I, and who received additional training by Ms. Rugh and others in various workshop and informal settings. These are Harvey and Arlyn Becker and Debbie Goldman.

At the end of the ten-week period, both Mishpacha I and II elected to continue on a less frequent basis (approximately once per month). It is hoped that in the Fall of 1975, two more Mishpacha groups (Mishpacha III and IV) will be formed with the Beckers leading one and a family in Mishpacha II leading the other.

Below is the transcript of a conversation centered around the experiences of one family in Mishpacha II, Robert and Susanne Cohen and their children, Caroline, 13, and Alan, 8. Also participating are Rabbi Dov Peretz Elkins and Phyllis Kasdin, chairperson of the Family Life Council.

The discussion follows.

MISHPACHA

This is Rabbi Dov Peretz Elkins of Temple Beth El, Rochester, New York. We are discussing this evening our Mishpacha program. Temple Beth El started an inter-generational family cluster, substitute extended family program about two years ago. One group came into existence in January 1974 and the second group in January 1975. In the second group was the Cohen family who are with me here tonight, Susanne and Robert Cohen and their children, Alan, 8, and Caroline, 13,. Also with us is Phyllis Kasdin, the chairperson of the Family Life Council of Temple Beth El, which sponsors the Family Life Program.

Robert, can you tell us something of your needs which brought you into the Mishpacha?

Robert Cohen: Susanne and I and our two children live in Rochester, New York, far from our immediate family. We are a typical example of a new and growing phenomenon called the nuclear family. We have friends in Rochester, enjoy a good social life, but we felt something definitely missing in terms of the richness of our Jewish life, and the sense of shared religious experience, in particular around the Jewish holidays, seders. We have friends who are not religiously oriented but are more social. We joined Temple Beth El, but it has the usual programs connected with a very, very large Temple and the inevitable sense of anonymity. We were happy to hear of Rabbi Elkins' suggestion for the Havurah groups which he presented at the Yom Kippur service (1973). Our original motivation was to get together with people who had similar religious interests and we have found this to be very, very satisfactory.

Rabbi Elkins: Alan, what was your idea when you heard about the Mishpacha—did you look forward to it, were you fearful about it, what did you think it was going to be?

Alan: I thought it was going to be really fun and I couldn't wait until I was going. I was jumping up and down. I didn't know what it was going to be like. My mother and father were going to a Mishpacha—what is that? I wasn't so keen on going. My mother explained what it was all about and it was really fantastic, I was jumping up and down.

Rabbi Elkins: Did it turn out the way you thought it would be? Are you happy being a member of the Mishpacha? Do you look forward to going to the meetings?

Alan: Yes, I love to go to the meetings.

Rabbi Elkins: What do you like the best?

Alan: Playing games and making things.

Rabbi Elkins: Caroline, what about you? What do you like about the Mishpacha, or don't like?

Caroline Cohen: For me it worked out more like a big family. There were two other girls approximately my age so I had lots of fun playing with them and whenever we went to these activities I could always talk with them and enjoy it with somebody.

Rabbi Elkins: Do you think the Mishpacha made you a better Jew in any way, Caroline? Any special Jewish things you enjoyed?

Caroline Cohen: We had a big Sabbath dinner together, but we always have Sabbath in our house.

Rabbi Elkins: Susanne, how about you: What does the Mishpacha mean to you?

Susanne Cohen: I don't know if I can talk about what it means to me. I can tell you what I experienced. I experienced seven different families and all kinds of different personalities who, more or less, have the same kinds of needs of getting closer to people who share a certain kind of view. We wanted to participate more in a Jewish way, in a religious way. We wanted to feel closer to people. We all felt that we missed something with our friends—a certain kind of shared Jewish experience, especially with children. Many of us have friends with couples and we don't participate with children in Jewish things.

Rabbi Elkins: What about the Jewish components?

Susanne Cohen: The first three or four meetings were getting to know people and the religious aspect was not emphasized. Then we did what we thought was a mitzva and that was to put on a program of music and dance at the Old Age Home in Rochester. That motivation probably came from our Jewish feeling of doing something worthwhile for ourselves and also for the people that we met there. In that sense, it was Jewish. When the holidays came, we talked about the holidays but I don't know how many of us are tremendously educated

(Jewishly) so that what we shared was a vague kind of knowledge rather than a deeper kind of knowledge. We had two Shabbat dinners and they were wonderful experiences. There is a different kind of feeling when you have other people other than your family. There is a different spirit that envelopes the group and I think it happened both times—a certain kind of warmth. Lots of people together sharing something that meant something. We read from the prayer-book. We just felt good.

Robert Cohen: My own personal feeling is that I very much enjoyed the Shabbat dinners. There was a warmth and comraderie and you got the feeling of how it must have been in some former, simpler time. Perhaps this is a *Fiddler on the Roof* type of nostalgia, but nevertheless I just started feeling a family in the true sense of the word, an extended family.

Rabbi Elkins: Robert, you are a scientist at Xerox which is a large corporation with a lot of people. It would seem to me that in a corporation like that, one might find that kind of comraderie, extended family relationships that a person always seeks. Obviously that is not the case for you, is that right?

Robert Cohen: In Xerox, I have many friends and colleagues. I would say that we have a certain kind of comraderie but in the synagogue you can find a base for shared Jewish living. The Mishpacha was a group of families chosen, not at random. It was a spectrum of ages. It was an attempt at some kind of structure. We all had the feeling of wanting to enrich our Jewish family life and that you can't pick up from any other type of organization. It is much too spotty.

Rabbi Elkins: Were there any side benefits of being in the Mishpacha outside the weekly meetings? You had a contract to meet for ten consecutive Sunday evenings initially—from about 5 to 7:30-8:00 p.m.—after which you elected to continue on a monthly or bi-monthly basis.

During those ten weeks were there any side benefits in any way in which the five or six families in the Mishpacha got together or did anything for each other in any way afterwards?

Robert Cohen: During the ten weeks, nobody really saw each other outside the group. There was a point when you began to feel closer and things began to happen in a more personal way outside the group.

Susanne Cohen: Like everything else, it evolved and I would say that about the fourth, fifth meeting when we decided to put on a program at the Jewish Home, I think we so-called lost ourselves in the process. That means we took off our social outer clothing and we got busy doing something for somebody else. Then you began to see the other people more as themselves rather than as their social selves. Their tastes, preferences came out. Their ways of doing things came out and you began to see them as fuller persons. That was a very important part of our development. We reached out beyond ourselves. After that time I think I found myself in conversations with individual people, talking about things that had nothing to do with Mishpacha. It just evolved—a sort of friendship. One Shabbat dinner, while everyone was cleaning up, three of us sat outside on the steps and began to talk about just family kind of things—sisters and brothers. Later when we came in the others who were working glared at us, rightly so. I quickly grabbed the vacuum cleaner to show that my intent was good and cleaned up the few crumbs that were left. That was to sort of balance the ledger, so to speak. That's when those types of relationships started to make little inroads. Because essentially we were strangers—seven families who never saw each other. We didn't have common experiences—maybe have people work at the same jobs and build up a relationship that way and then invite them over socially. It is a difficult kind of thing to have people sort-of thrown together. You need the commitment, you need the ten weeks. That's the structure that allows whatever is going to happen to happen. We were fortunate in having some things happen. I would say that we began to see people as they really are. After ten weeks, and even after that, certain things about people irritate one another, and we began to see it, to experience it. But we had a backlog of good feeling toward these people so that when some of their less splendid traits were shown we didn't really mind that much. We tried to help them rather than criticize them.

Rabbi Elkins: They were members of your "family" and you had to accept them as they really were.

Susanne Cohen: Right. At the end of the ten week meeting, the people who ran the Mishpacha (Facilitators) put a tremendous amount of work into the Mishpacha. They really went beyond the call of duty. Then toward the end, they wanted to give the reins to other people, but they didn't know quite how to do it. They were very sensitive and very on edge. They acted like they were hurt and put upon. Instead of us reacting "against them" because they weren't acting social, we all tried to understand and offer our hand in comforting words and we sat and talked.

Rabbi Elkins: They had their agenda and the group wanted to do something else and there was friction. The group understood where they were coming from and talked it out and got over it.

Susanne Cohen: The main thing was the way in which the friction was handled. It was not handled in a neutral way, in an indifferent way. It was handled in a way that we care about these people. These people worked very, very hard for the group. Perhaps they are showing a limitation on their personality; perhaps they were tired. I don't know what it was. We didn't really care what it was. What we cared about was having the group continue and to iron out the differences.

Rabbi Elkins: Susanne, you said before that after the ten weeks there was an experience that was particularly meaningful to you about the Bat Mitzvah. Can you tell us about that?

Susanne Cohen: My daughter was going to be Bat Mitzvah April eleventh. I unfortunately did not do as much preparation for her Bat Mitzvah as was necessary. None of my close friends had bat mitzvahs or bar mitzvahs and I was never involved with their preparations so I miscalculated the amount of time and effort that was necessary to have a Bat Mitzvah that would be beautiful, meaningful and on time. Since I was doing a great deal of the cooking, and since it was going to be in my home, there were many details to attend to. The month of March vanished. Pesah, my children had chicken pox and we all had piano auditions and had to play for a piano judge, a piece by memory. March vanished and April appeared. We had a snow storm on one of Rochester's lucky weekends and my husband took off for two weeks across the country. There I was with two children, a car that leaked gasoline, and the Bat Mitzvah that would appear in three or four weeks. I panicked and one of the women called me and asked if I was going to come to a meeting. I said no I couldn't come and spilled out a small piece of my turmoil. She tried to comfort me. This was the eldest couple. Her name is Harriet and she has children in their twenties and she tried to put things in their perspective and tell me it all works out—comforting kind of things. She sounded like a member of the family who had been through it and had an experience that she wanted to share with me. The following day, Sunday, my daughter, Caroline, was in a recital. She had to be at the piano teacher at 4:30. The Mishpacha meeting was at 5:30 at a vegetarian restaurant. I wasn't going to go but since the piano recital had ended early, I wasn't going to go home to make dinner so I decided to go to the Mishpacha meeting, which I did. We had a miserable dinner—"unburger"—soy bean (pareve) kind of burger. But I really didn't care what I was eating. It was just nice to be with people. After that one of the women suggested that we come to her home. At her home, as I sat on her soft couch, I poured out, to their astonishment, my feelings of helplessness at this Bat Mitzvah that was looming in front of me. They all, almost in unison, started to say that they were going to help. They were going to help with the cooking and in any other way they could. What emerged was a solid support, a human support for me and the fear, the helplessness, the aloneness that I experienced, even though I had other close friends, who said they were going to help me, but the fact that they all said it together—face to face, nose to nose—gave me a feeling that I could go home and I could start without feeling so worried. That human experience allowed me to start the mechanical business of running around to find out where I'm going to buy my flowers and where I am going to buy other things. They also helped in a tangible way. I borrowed all their silver, glassware, and all kinds of really valuable things that they were very willing to lend me. I was able to use all of their things. I served fifty-five people with all their serving things. They brought different things like jello molds, a jar of pickles. The food really wasn't that important . . .

Rabbi Elkins: It turned out to be a real substitute family for you. Saved your life. Robert, can you put this in perspective for us in terms of what you were telling me some weeks ago about having moved here. You consider yourself a kind of corporate type of individual who gets transferred from city to city and it is hard to strike really deep roots and feel familiness. How does the Mishpacha affect all of that?

Robert Cohen: As I mention to you, Rabbi, earlier, I came from the Bronx where being Jewish was in the air. When Pesah came, we dressed in our finest, went out on the main avenue, and all the stores were closed. I remember as a child, much to my dismay, all the candy stores were closed. It was only after I left New York did I feel more of a sense of isolation because I didn't have the support of the Jewish community.

Rabbi Elkins: How long have you been in Rochester?

Robert Cohen: Nearly eight years. Just before Susanne and I and the family came to Rochester, we lived in a small town in New Jersey, about 30 miles west of the Holland Tunnel. There we started our synagogue affiliation and joined a small Conservative temple in Summit, N.J. Their sense of Jewish isolation was typified by the fact that they were called the Jewish Community Center. It wasn't even called a temple. The feeling of closeness we had there was very memorable. We had a group of the Bell Telephone Laboratories which would meet every Wednesday night. We had a little cheder to study Humash. That came to an end when I received a better job at Xerox and we came to Rochester and I joined Temple Beth El. There I found quite a different story. It was not a little Conservative shtibel. It was a huge beautiful synagogue and it needed to be compartmentalized and I felt a lack of community. I wasn't encouraged and after a while I quit. I returned later. The highlight of our return was joining the Mishpacha and my daughter's Bat Mitzvah. Two wonderful events for us. While the Mishpacha, imperfect in many ways, started to resurrect the feelings of both my extended community of the Bronx and also that close feeling of the little Conservative shtibel in New Jersey. The synagogue simply must be compartmentalized. People cannot interact in a massive way. Something distinct from social friends which are usually along the lines of couples, try to make friends with a variety of people. Here we have a group that is dedicated to trying to enrich each other's Jewish family life.

Rabbi Elkins: Alan, do you have grandparents?

Alan: I have one grandpa and two grandmas.

Rabbi Elkins: Do you find the Mishpacha is a good substitute when they are not around?

Alan: Yes.

Susanne Cohen: We spent a lot of minutes talking about the religious aspects. The truth of the matter is that in this Mishpacha, at least now, in terms of the meetings we've had, most of them were not directed mainly toward a religious experience. The 20th of June, the Mishpacha is going on a camping trip with all of the families. Somebody in the group happens to like camping very much. There are some who have never gone on a camping trip. So it is a shared human experience, especially for city folks, to go out into the woods and sleep under the stars. In the fall we thought we might go to Buffalo to visit the Chabad house which is a Hasidic center in Buffalo. That will be a religious experience.

Rabbi Elkins: You recited the Birkat HaMazon after every meal at Mishpacha meetings. Did it have any effect at home?

Susanne Cohen: Not yet. Only in the sense that I have a copy of it now. We bought the books, Likrat Shabbat, which is a marvelous book and we now use that book every Shabbat for singing songs, reading various readings. We always said kiddush but not Birkat HaMazon. We are inching up to it.

Rabbi Elkins: One session of the Mishpacha was to write your own version of Birkat HaMazon, what you wanted to pray for.

Caroline: May the all merciful—I don't remember what it was exactly—something about Russia. May the all merciful bless and keep Israel and may Russia platz. (laughter)

Rabbi Elkins: Phyllis, let me ask you something from the Temple's point of view. Has the Mishpacha added anything to the Temple structure itself, such as increased Shabbat attendance or a closer tie to the Temple on the part of the members? Do you see any benefit for the Temple apart from the personal thing?

Phyllis Kasdin: There have only been fourteen or fifteen families, thus far, involved in the Mishpacha, but I do believe that these families do come to synagogue more now than they did before they were members of the Mishpacha. Also the group met at the Temple each week. The program brought them into the building and they began to feel more at home in the building; other than Hebrew school or services. In this way, it definitely has enhanced the Temple and because the two groups have been so successful word has gotten out to the other congregants and we have many applications to start more groups and hopefully we will start more in the Fall.

Rabbi Elkins: Where do you think we ought to go from here in your Mishpacha? Is it going to be continuing, have you all had enough? What exactly does the future have in store for you?

Robert Cohen: Susanne alluded to our last meeting in which she alluded to some friction with the co-facilitators. At that point, we made a fundamental decision about our identity. There were two distinct paths we could take. In fact, they represented the dichotomy that was present in the two co-facilitators. One direction to go was more social with or without children involved in various activities, evenings together, more in terms of "talking to one another," in the sense of probing, getting to know one another more intimately, contact, more sensitivity-type of orientations without the formalities of the sensitivity games. The other direction was to keep it purely a family cluster and to do things totally with the family. To have it social but not in the orientation that I just mentioned and to concentrate on family activities and religious activities. We chose the latter and therefore had a thorough thrashing out of our identities. We all have a much better feeling about it. We all want to continue. There were some disagreements about the frequency of our meetings. Susanne and I wanted to meet less often than most others. The only thing we felt about the ten weeks was it seemed to be very demanding of our time, but looking back on it, I think it was certainly rewarding because you can't be impatient with a delicate process. But we all are agreed to continue meeting and to continue with a family cluster identity. In that sense there is no ambiguity. I think I see our group growing, becoming used to each other. We will have a sukkah together next year, a seder and we may do something together on the minor Jewish holidays.

Susanne Cohen: The name of the group is Mishpacha (family) and we brought it out in previous comments. Mishpacha means family and family means acceptance of people, for the good, not so good, and even the negative. I think what emerged from our Mishpacha was an acceptance of people's limitations without the pointing of a critical finger. We said, all of us, that this one maybe is too critical, this one is too uptight or this one is too withdrawn. That's what they were, but in spite of it, we still accepted them and we worked around it, aside it, and this is the special quality of the Mishpacha, because many times when you are with a group of people, even on a social level, if they don't show you their splendid personality and the really good parts of themselves, their value goes down in your eyes and you think to yourself, I'm not going to see them anymore because they don't act this way, and they don't do this, etc. But, in the Mishpacha, if people didn't do what you expected them to do and didn't act the way you expected them to act, or even say what you expected them to say, we still decided emotionally, in an unsaid way, that it was O.K. That's very important. Yes, I am looking forward to it. My main interest is a more religious one. I would like to participate more deeply in the Jewish holidays and to learn much more. I like a more intellectual approach, more learning. In a group like this with so many different kinds of people, so many different interests, there are many ways of learning. You can learn through books or you can learn through experiencing. You can go through many doors that don't say learning on them, but you come out having learned something.

Caroline Cohen: I don't want to change anything. I like it the way it is going. As my father mentioned before, he and my mother didn't want to meet as frequently as all the other people; some wanted to meet once a week which is a little too much. My parents wanted to meet once a month or every month and a half or so. I think every two weeks or three weeks would be good because you still have a feeling of connection— you can look forward to—it's a long time but you don't get bored of their actions. I have nice friends and we do nice things, too.

Alan: The day we were supposed to end the Mishpacha, we were in a big circle and we were talking about ending the Mishpacha or not. Most everyone said once a month, but Sheila Markowitz, who was the last, said more often—every week. I agreed with her. I liked the Shabbat dinner. We had one in Arlyn's place and in our place because we have a big house and we had lots of fun.

Rabbi Elkins: I think this is a good place to stop. Thanks everybody.

8
The Havurah Program

by Phyllis Kasdin, *Chairperson*
Family Life Council
Temple Beth El, Rochester, New York

In an effort to foster warmth and friendliness among the 1300 member families of Temple Beth El, Rabbi Elkins suggested that Havurah groups be instituted. As a result of the large number of congregants, it became difficult for members to met each other and many complained of a cold, impersonal atmosphere. Rabbi Elkins felt if we could, in some way, break the congregation into smaller groups, a warmer, more inviting atmosphere would be created.

The first step was to inaugurate a Family Life Council. This Council, in addition to sponsoring the Havurot, also sponsored Mishpachah groups and various other activities and programs dealing with family life.

The concept of Havurah was first introduced through Rabbi Elkins' sermons on Rosh Hashanah and Yom Kippur, 1973. Shortly after the holidays, a questionnaire was sent to each family of the congregation, inviting them to join a Havurah. The questionnaire was simple and direct, asking such information as age category, number and age of children, whether they want to be in a group with mixed ages or their own age group, and whether they want an emphasis on study or social activity.

Initially, about 150 applications came back. A chairperson of Havurot was chosen and she, along with the chairperson of the Family Life Council and the Rabbi, reviewed the applications and formed the groups. Because of the many varied requests, it was impossible to group the applicants, taking into consideration all their preferences. It was finally decided to group people at random, taking into consideration only whether they wanted to be in a mixed age group or the same age group. Ten groups were formed, one of those in their twenties, three in their thirties, one in their forties, one in their fifties, one sixty and over and three mixed age groups.

One couple was selected from each group to act as coordinator of the group. It was their responsibility initially to call the first meeting and get the group going. It was hoped that once the group was organized, the leadership would rotate. A meeting of the coordinators was called and they were given a short briefing in group dynamics, suggestions for programs and a talk on what the objectives of Havurah should be.

The leaders were urged not to get into any sort of encounter groups or deep psychological experiences or experiments. This was not the objective of Havurah. Rather, the objective was to serve as an extended family. In this age of mobility, there is a crying need for family type relationships. The leaders were given the lists of their members, a list of rules and regulations for Havurah and urged to call the group meeting as soon as possible. The coordinators were also told not to reveal the names of the other group members, even if asked, in order to avoid apprehensions by some people. Each person was asked to stick with the Havurah group assigned for one year. At the end of the year, if they desired, they could be switched into another group.

Within a month of the coordinators meeting, each group had met and, for the most part, gotten off to a flying start.

There were some problems, such as whether to study or socialize and whether to involve total families in programming or keep it strictly couples. For the most part, a happy balance was found and each group developed its own peculiar characteristics. At first, surprisingly enough, the mixed age groups were highly successful with the homogeneous age groups having slightly more difficulty in programming. By the end of the year, however, though the mixed age groups were still going strong, some couples asked to be transferred into groups with couples their own age. We attribute this to the fact that these couples were looking for more social contacts within their own age group and were not achieving this in the mixed group.

Very exciting things happened within each group. The groups usually met once a month at a different member's home. Programs varied from learning Israeli dances, to studying Hassidism, to family picincs. One group had a Passover Seder together. Many groups held an Oneg Shabbat together. Most groups attended Selihot services together. Many came as groups to Temple functions such as Sisterhood's Hanukah Dinner and Purim Ball and the Temple's annual dinner meeting. Many of these people admit they would never attend these functions alone, but because they came with a Havurah group, they felt warm and welcome and developed a sense of belonging. Bar Mitzvahs and Brises and times of mourning were also shared within each group. The family feeling we had hoped to foster was generally created. Surprisingly enough, few personality conflicts developed.

The Rabbi, as well as the officers of the congregation, made themselves available to speak to each group, which they did on more than one occasion.

By January, there were enough new people requesting Havurah groups to form a new group. These people were grouped simply because they were late in sending in an application. This group has turned out to be extremely successful and the members have become very close.

One of the most successful groups is the one composed of newly marrieds. These are couples in their twenties anxious to develop some Jewish commitment. They were all strangers before Havurah and have developed a cohesive group, anxious to participate in Temple functions and study Judaism as well as enjoy each other. They held one of their Havurah meetings in conjunction with the Havurah in the sixties age category and a very interesting dialogue and exchange of ideas took place. Both groups consider this one of the highlights of their season.

Every few months, coordinators meetings were held with the Rabbi and chairperson of Havurah and Family Life Council to evaluate each group, exchange program ideas and evaluate the Havurah program as a whole. By the end of the season, early June, it was concluded that the Havurah program had had a successful year. It was then decided to hold a social function for all Havurah members. A square dance was held at the Temple in August and that too was highly successful. Over 100 people attended and all agreed it was probably one of the warmest, most friendly and fun evenings held at Temple Beth El. Since the party was on a Saturday night, the evening started with Havdalah and then proceeded into square dancing and ended with a lox and bagel midnight supper. At the end, each group told a little about their year and particularly at this time, the spirit of comraderie and closeness was most evident.

In July each member of the Temple family received another application to join a Havurah. We have just formed three new groups. A few people have dropped out of the program and new couples have been put into these groups to take their place. A few couples requested transfer into another group, but for the most part, the program is going strong and we are looking forward to another successful year.

QUESTIONNAIRE FOR HAVUROT

NAME_____ Marital Status:

     First   Last

Married _____

Spouse's Name (if applicable) _____ Widowed_____

Single _____

Address _____

                             Zip

Phone_____

Age Range: 20-25_____ 25-35_____ 35-45 _____ 45-55_____ 55-60_____
         Over 60_____

CHILDREN: NAMES   Sex   Age

_____

_____

Your goals in joining:

    Social Emphasis: Some_____ Frequent_____
    Study Emphasis: Some_____ Frequent_____

_____I/We are interested in becoming a Havurah co-ordinator
(Check one: Husband_____Wife_____Both_____)

_____I/We prefer to be with couples our own age (refer to age
range) _____.

_____I/We prefer a group with a wide age range.

Purpose of joining Havurah: _____

_____

I/we became interested in the Havurah through a) Temple
Bulletin_____ b) personal friends_____ c) other _____

Please return to: Havurah, Family Life Council, Temple Beth El,
               139 S. Winton Road, Rochester, New York 14610

TEMPLE BETH EL FAMILY LIFE COUNCIL

SUGGESTED HAVUROT ACTIVITIES

Friday night Oneg Shabbat or Dinner
Campout
Lecture (invite anyone on Temple staff, or outsider)
Songfest
Havdalah (Saturday night)
Service project for the Temple (Speak to Harry Albert or Rabbi)
Hanukah Party, Purim Party, etc.
Weekend to New York, Grossingers, etc.
Pesach Seder
Visit a Church or other Community organization
Visit a religious service, wedding, of another faith

Add your own suggestions here:

_____

_____

_____

_____
_____
_____
_____
_____
_____
_____

TEMPLE BETH EL FAMILY LIFE COUNCIL
SUGGESTED DISCUSSION THEMES FOR HAVUROT

1. Rites of Passages (birth, bar/bat mitzvah, marriage, death and mourning) Hayyim Schauss, THE LIFETIME OF A JEW; Code of Jewish Law.
2. The Book of Job (BOOK OF GOD AND MAN by Robert Gordis; ANSWER TO JOB by Carl Jung; THE DIMENSIONS OF JOB, ed. N. Glatzer; J.B. by Archibald Macleish; JOB STANDS UP by Michael Gelber, UAHC).
3. Israel and World Politics (sources are endless)
4. Jews and Arabs Throughout History (JEWS AND ARABS, Goitein)
5. Great Jewish Personalities (B'nai B'rith paperback by same title)
6. Great Jewish Thinkers of 20th Century (B'nai B'rith paperback by same title)
7. Contemporary Jewish Thought (B'nai B'rith paperback)
8. Great Jewish Ideas (B'nai B'rith paperback)
9. Jewish Theology and Philosophy (FAITH FOR MODERNS by Robert Gordis paperback)
10. Current Jewish Problems (based on monthly issues of magazines like THE JEWISH SPECTATOR, COMMENTARY, SHMA, etc.)
11. The Writings of Mordecai M. Kaplan, Founder of Reconstructionism (Many different paperback books available)
12. Understanding Ourselves and Others (GAMES PEOPLE PLAY by Eric Berne)
13. Enriching our Marriage (MY BELOVED IS MINE by Rabbi Roland Gittelsohn)
14. Soviet Jewry (Many paperbacks available)
15. Judaism and Social Action (JUDAISM AND SOCIAL CRISIS, Albert Vorspan)
16. Great Jewish Books (Paperback of same title, Ribalow and Caplan)

9
The Worship Service: New Horizons

NEW PRAYERS

1. One of the most productive sources for innovative prayers and prayer books is Media Judaica, Inc., 1363 Fairfield Avenue, Bridgeport, Conn. 06605. Write for their full catalogue.

Some of the materials from Media Judaica which I find particularly useful are: Likrat Shabbat, "Contemporary Prayers and Readings," "New Prayers for High Holy Days," "For Modern Minds and Hearts," and "Rejoice with Jerusalem."

2. Cf. *The Mahzor,* edited by Jules Harlow (The Rabbinical Assembly). Those congregations who do not opt for the new RA mahzor can benefit from it by having the rabbi read some of its new readings from the pulpit.

3. For fifteen dollars, one can subscribe to the Creative Service Project of Rabbi Harry Essrig, and receive good sermons and interesting creative services all year long. Write to Rabbi Harry Essrig, 444 Tuallitan Road, Los Angeles, Calif. 90049.

4. Write to Sacred Design, 840 Colorado Avenue S., Minneapolis, Minn. 55416 for beautifully executed covers and booklets for the High Holidays.

5. A very valuable book with new readings, often used by Unitarians, for such occasions as birth, coming-of-age (Bar/Bat Mitzvah), marriage and death, is *Great Occasions,* edited by Carl Seaburg (Beacon Press, $10, 1968).

Presented at the Rabbinical Assembly Convention, May 5-9, 1974.

6. More and more young couples are asking to add their own readings to the traditional wedding service, especially after "Love Story." Very helpful for this purpose is a book edited by our colleague, Rabbi Mordecai Brill (et al.), called *Write Your Own Wedding* (*Association Press*, $2.95, paper).

7. Often colleagues will want to put together a devotional responsive reading for a special occasion in the congregation and/or community. This is easily done by consulting several excellent Jewish anthologies, and consulting a particular heading, such as "education," "love," or "truth." Some good anthologies that can be used for this purpose are *Treasury in the Art of Living, Modern Treasury of Jewish Thoughts, Rabbinic Anthology, Talmudic Anthology,* and *Hasidic Anthology.*

8. Hillel Foundations often are in the forefront of liturgical experimentation. Some of it has been written up in a booklet published by the B'nai B'rith Hillel Foundation edited by Alfred Jospe, "Worship in the Hillel Foundations."

9. Another collection of Hillel oriented and originated liturgical materials is a book called *Bridges to a Holy Time,* edited by Alfred Jospe and Richard N. Levy (Ktav, 1972).

10. Several new books have been published by Abingdon Press, Nashville, Tenn., 37202, on innovations in liturgy. Some of these are:

    a. *Contemporary Celebration* by Ross Snyder, $4.75. Concerned with "intensifying realness, immediacy, presence, warmth, momentum, expectancy and surprise and astonishment and awe in church events."

    b. *New Forms of Worship* by James F. White, $5.75. Explores influence of such elements are architecture, non-verbal communication, sights and sounds, multi-media worship, new preaching methods.

    c. *Awakened Worship,* Involving Laymen in Creative Worship, by Wilfred M. Bailey, $2.95 (paper). (Good bibliography on page 157.)

11. In some congregations (not yours, of course), intransigent ritual committees need persuasion of the historical flexibility of Jewish liturgy. For this purpose, I have reprinted and distributed copies of an excellent article by our colleague, Rabbi Herman Kieval, "Prayer—the Need for Revision," from The Torch, Summer/Fall, 1971, pages 27-31.

12. A contemporary and very germane prayer in regard to Watergate has been composed, called "Prayer for Government" by Rabbi Albert Axelrad. Write to Brandeis University Hillel Foundation.

13. I highly recommend an excellent article stressing the need for increasing *emotion, mystery,* and *drama* in the service. "Winds of Liturgical Reform," by Edward Graham, in *Judaism,* Winter, 1974, pp. 52-60.

I often use lay people for dramatic readings, and when accused of turning the pulpit into a theatre, I point out that the *traditional* services, both in the ancient Temple and in the synagogues, are filled with highly dramatic moments, such as kohen gadol on Yom Kippur in Holy of Holies, in the Temple; and in the synagogue, marching around with the Torah, standing before ark, calling up seven congregants to say blessings over the Torah reading. (Were we to suggest calling up seven men from the congregation to say blessings and/or read the Torah, it would surely be called a "gimmick."

14. Some congregations are now re-introducing the Birkat Kohanim (duchaning) on the shalosh regalim, as an example of a high dramatic ritual in the service.

15. In the Birkat HaMazon, there is much room for creativity in the HaRachaman section. Three I add invariably are: (a) HaRachaman, hu yevarech et medinat yisrael, raysheet tzemichat geulatenu; (b) HaRachaman, hu yevarech et achaynu bet yisrael ha-netunim be-tzara, ve-yotzee-aym may afayla le-ora; (c) HaRachaman, hu yevarech et chayalay tzva hagana le-yisrael, ve-yachzeeraym be-shalom. (The last one has been used in Isreal since the Yom Kippur War.

Also in the HaRachaman section, I add the names of all the members of my family, and anyone else sitting at our table: HaRachaman, hu yevarech otee, et ishtee Ilana, et bni Hillel, et bni Yonatan, et beetee Shira, . . . otanu ve-chol asher lanu, kmo she-nitbarchu . . . .

16. In the Yom Kippur Martyrology, I substitute a modern reading for the traditional material. Examples: Milton Steinberg's "When I Think of Seraye," (in *A Believing Jew*); Yossele Rockover's Diary; Elie Wiesel - his piece on Yom Kippur in *Legends of Out Time.*

17. Rabbi Noah Golinkin will be happy to send you a copy of his catalogue of innovative liturgical materials.

NEW FORMATS

It is not only new prayers that have the power to give our services a sense of renewal and freshness. Sometimes the old prayers in a new setting, or with a new addition, can achieve the same effect. Below are some suggestions for new *formats* in liturgical innovation.

1. Robert Hammer's article in a past issue of BEINEINU, "Service Experiments." Individual worshippers rise from their seats at given times in the service, prearranged, and read short selections such as midrashim, a chasidic story, or a poem.
2. Harold Schulweis, Friday night (Encino, Calif.): people come to the auditorium where they get in the mood for prayers by singing hasidic songs and clapping vigorously. When most worshippers have gathered, they march together, singing and clapping, to the sanctuary for the service.
3. Harold Kushner, Natick, Mass., has Oneg Shabbat *before* Friday night services, including singing and refreshments. This helps create a sense of community prior to the worship experience and permits late-comers to straggle in and not miss any of the service.
4. For Purim, many congregations have a full Megillah reading in the regular chapel service at 6 P.M. and a later family service about 7 or 7:30 P.M. Some of these include a Purim Spiel, awards for the best costume, after the children parade on the pulpit (all children are encouraged to come in costume). Religious School students read selections of the Megillah.
5. At Beth El, Rochester, we have done several innovative things on Simchat Torah. First, the Torah is read (in the evening) *before* the hakafot, instead of after (as is traditional), while people are calm and not overtired, and can listen with attentiveness.

More importantly, services are held on Simchat Torah night in the auditorium instead of in the main sanctuary. A bema can be set up in the middle, around which the hakafot take place. Chairs are set along the walls in a square. This permits maximum space for dancing. Other congregations include use of an accordion for the singing and dancing during hakafot to help bring a slight bit of order into the planned chaos.

6. For Yom Ha-Shoah many innovative formats are used. See the articles by Rabbi David Arzt, in a recent issue of BEINEINU, and Rabbi Robert A. Hammer, in an issue of the *United Synagogue Review*. Rabbi Samuel Dresner, Beth El, Highland Park, Ill., organized services in homes of the members in which *Night Words—A Midrash on the Holocaust* is read by thirty-six participants.

In Rochester, the Jewish Community Federation sent out a prayer with a cover letter suggesting that each family light a candle with the family gathered together on Erev Yom HaShoah.

Yom HaShoah services have been written by Rabbi Efry Spectre and Rabbi Raphael Ostrovsky.

In the military chaplaincy, I organized a service at which every entering worshiper was given a yellow arm band to pin on, with a magendavid and "Jude" written on it. Candles were lit by each person for holocaust victims.

7. Involvement of children at Shabbat services

a. Rabbi Hillel Silverman has a dialogue with teenagers from the pulpit on the sidrah of the week, near the end of the service.

b. At Beth El, Rochester, I sit on the steps of the pulpit before En Kelohenu, holding the microphone in my hand, and invite all pre-Bar/Bat Mitzvah children to come and sit on the steps with me. For three minutes we chat about something in the sidrah or other Jewish matter. The children sit through the service waiting for their big moment to come up.

c. Some congregations are re-introducing an'eem zemirot before Adon Olam, led by a child. It has a catchy, easily learned, and responsive chant.

8. Involvement of Women

a. Aliyot; haftara; opening ark; sermonettes during summer; bat mitzvah on Shabbat morning.

b. In prayers for baby-naming, illness, bar/bat mitzvah, bride and groom, use of both parents of the person blessed can be used (e.g., David ben Avraham ve-Sarah). In Israel, soldiers' tombstones all have both parents' names. Some suggest using the mother's name first and then the father's, in case father is a kohen or levi (e.g. David ben Sarah veAvraham Hakohen).

9. Bar/Bat Mitzvah ceremony

a. During the birkat kohanim, after my charge to bat mitzvah, I will place my hands on the head of the youngsters. Body contact makes the experience more meaningful, emotional.

b. Some colleagues, instead of the traditional charge, will have a dialogue with the child.

c. Some colleagues go down and stand with the family for the she-he-che-yanu and tallit ceremony.

10. Kiddush after Shabbat morning services.

This is often a problem because the rabbi and cantor get to the Kiddush table late, after shaking hands with dozens of congregants, and by that time everyone is anxious and hungry or they've already begun to gorge themselves without waiting for the bracha. At Beth El, we have the bar/bat mitzvah come up to the pulpit after adon olam and before the closing benediction to recite kiddush. Then the worshipers can proceed immediately to the kiddush table without waiting for anyone and the rabbi and cantor can leisurely wish "Shabbat Shalom" without rushing away.

11. Many innovative and lively melodies are being added to the Shabbat morning service to give it freshness and more life:

a. Shlomo Carlbach's En Kelohenu

b. Charles Davidson's Adon Olam from "Chassidic Sabbath" (FAMOUS RECORD - FAM-1006, recorded by Cantor Ray Smolover and Choir)

c. Festival Torah Service used at Adath Jeshurun, Elkins Park, Pa.

10
The Liturgy Explosion

"Innovate something each day in your prayers," admonishes the Talmud. The fear of having the traditional "stamp of prayer," the fixed liturgy, become mechanical, dry and meaningless, was one which the ancient rabbis shared long before prayer book reform in the nineteenth and twentieth century. Rabbi Hayyim Kieval demonstrated in a cogent article several years ago that changing the siddur and adding new prayers is a very old custom among pious Jews. Much more so than we who love the old melodies of En Kelohenu would like to think ("Prayer—The Need for Revision," *Torch,* Summer/Fall, 1971, pages 27-31).

Within the past few years, a number of extremely important developments have taken place in Jewish houses of prayer which augur well for the future of meaningful prayer in Judaism. These include the creation of new prayers and of new formats in worship.

NEW PRAYERS

In the category of new prayers are two significant collections of traditional and innovative prayers which are used

Published in Women's League *Outlook,* Spring, 1976.

widely today in Conservative congregations. *Likrat Shabbat,* edited by Rabbi Sidney Greenberg (Media Judaica, 1973), is designed for use at Friday night services. It contains the entire traditional Friday night service, but interspersed between each two traditional prayers are five to seven pages of new prayers. This gives the congregation the opportunity to reflect on some of the meanings of the hoary Hebrew words as enunciated in modern English expressions. It also supplies several possible innovative prayers for alternating in a cycle of four Sabbaths, so that each Friday night in one month different readings can be employed without repetition.

In the early part of Likrat Sabbat one finds this stirring midrash on "Mah Tovu" (page 17):

> May the door of this synagogue be wide enough
> to receive all who hunger for love,
> all who are lonely for fellowship . . . .
>
> May the door of this synagogue be narrow enough
> to shut out pettiness and pride, envy, and emnity.
>
> May its threshold be no stumbling block
> to young or straying feet.
>
> May it be too high to admit complacency,
> selfishness, and harshness.
>
> May this synagogue be, for all who enter,
> the doorway to a richer and more meaningful life.

An alternative version of the evening prayer, *Hashkeevenu,* reads as follows (page 92):

> Help us, O God, to lie down in peace;
> But teach us that peace means more than quiet.
>
> Remind us that if we are to be at peace at night,
> We must take heed how we live by day.

Grant us the peace that comes from honest dealing,
So that no fear of discovery will haunt our sleep.

Rid us of resentments and hatreds
Which rob us of the peace we crave.

Liberate us from enslaving habits
Which disturb us and give us no rest.

May we inflict no pain, bring no shame,
And seek no profit by another's loss.

The other prayer book used widely in our congregations is Rabbi Jules Harlow's new *Mahzor for Rosh Hashanah and Yom Kippur* (The Rabbinical Assembly, 1972). Extremely attractive in layout, each page is boxed by a royal purple square, symbolizing God's kingship, the theme of the Days of Awe. The Torah and Haftara readings are printed in the Hebrew script of the beautiful Koren Bible and those pages used only on Shabbat are bleached with a light purple background.

The Yom Kippur confessional, *ashamnu*, an alphabetical acrostic in Hebrew, is made to follow the alphabet in English as well: We abuse, we betray, we are cruel, we destroy, we embitter, we falsify, and so on. While the new RA Mahzor follows the traditional format very closely, a few modern Hebrew prayers are included. One by the late Hebrew poet and Jewish Theological Seminary professor, Hillel Bavli, is included on page 412 in the Yom Kippur evening service, in the original and in English translation:

> Let me not swerve from my life's path,
> Let not my spirit wither and shrivel
> In its thirst for You
> And lose the dew
> With which You sprinkled it
> When I was young.

May my heart be open
To every broken soul,
To orphaned life,
To every stumbler
Wandering unknown
And groping in the shadow.

Bless my eyes, purify me to see
Man's beauty rise in the world . . . .

And when my time comes—
Let me slip into the night
Demanding nothing, God, of man,
Or of You.

Most moving of all the innovations in the Harlow Mahzor is the arrangement of the Kaddish in the Martyrology (page 567), with the name of cities and places where Jews were slaughtered interspersed after each word of the mourner's Doxology. (For example: Yitagel - Kishinev; veyitkadash - Warsaw; shmay rabba - Auschwitz). In our congregation, Temple Beth El of Rochester, the Hazzan chants each word of the Kaddish solemnly, and after each Aramaic word the choir recites in unison the name of the place that follows the traditional word in the Mahzor. It is one of the most moving moments of the High Holy Day experience.

Many other rabbis are trying their hand at creative services and innovative prayer offerings. For lack of space, I can only list some of them: Rabbi Harry Essrig of Los Angeles has a "Creative Service Project" that invites subscribers to pay twenty dollars annually for monthly mailings of new and different religious services. Rabbi Bernard Raskas of Minneapolis has created some beautifully executed designs for his creative prayer collections. The B'nai B'rith Hillel Foundations has published *Bridges To a Holy Time* which includes some of the new things coming out of the Jewish services on the campuses.

While much of the new material is useful, much of it is also stale and dry and lacking the crucial emotional touch. In a recent article in *Judaism* (Winter, 1974, pages 52-60), Edward Graham issues a plea for more emotion, mystery, and drama in our services. Surely the service of the Kohen Gadol wearing his special white vestments, entering the Holy of Holies on the most sacred day of the year created a high pitch of drama and excitement. No one aware of this tradition can accuse modernists of overacting.

Interestingly, the Birkat HaMazon's Harachaman section is the beneficiary of many contemporary additions. These include special prayers for the welfare of the State of Israel and its brave defenders, for persecuted Jews behind the Iron Curtain and in Arab lands, and for other personal petitions. The wedding ceremony is another popular object of the creative muse, with young brides and grooms more frequently requesting not only music from *Love Story* but poetry from Khalil Gibran, and sometimes wearing simple white clothing in the field or by the lake. One talented groom, accompanying himself on the guitar, sang a song adapted from "Wanderlove" by Mason Williams:

> Come my love and we shall wander
> All of life to see and know.
> In our journey's lost wood rambling,
> Seasons come and seasons go.

Whereupon the bride sang:

> Come my love and we shall wander,
> Just to see what we can find.
> If we only find each other,
> Still the journey's worth the time.

(See *Write Your Own Wedding* edited by Mordecai Brill and others, Association Press; and *The Wedding Book* by Howard Kirschenbaum & Rockwell Stensrud, Seabury).

I now include this benediction in every wedding ceremony at which I officiate, taking into consideration some of the new ideas about women's rights to be recognized as persons apart from their husbands:

> May God's love ever be turned in your direction.
> May He grant you a life of collective fulfillment
>   as husband and wife,
> Individual fulfillment as woman and man,
> Health, happiness and peace.
>
> May the blessings which you will share in the
>   days and years ahead be blessings in
> which all may share,
> So that we may be blessed by your blessings.

INNOVATIVE FORMATS

In addition to the new prayers and prayerbooks being used in modern congregations, there are new formats which, while no new words are added, give a sense of relevance and freshness to the worship experience.

In some synagogues, a worshiper will rise from his seat and read a poem, a midrash, and a hasidic story. Elsewhere, as in Encino, California, the congregation gathers first in the auditorium for a mood-setting song, then marches to the sanctuary while clapping. In Natick, Massachusetts, the Oneg Shabbat is held *before* Friday night services to help create a sense of religious community as preparation to meaningful prayer.

In my congregation, we have held Simchat Torah services in the auditorium where there is more room for dancing and frenzied celebration over the Torah. We also invite the pre-Bar/Bat Mitzvah children to the pulpit before En Kelohenu every Shabbat morning while I sit on the *bema* steps and chat with them for a few minutes. We have recently begun calling the B'nai Mitzvah by their own Hebrew name of that of *both* their parents (David ben Sarah ve-Chaim). In still other communities, the long-discarded *duchan* ceremony is being restored, in which the Kohanim come up front with taletot over their heads to bless the congregation at the end of the Musaf Amida.

Similarly, An'eem Zemirot is being restored before Adon Olam, and is led by young children, or the younger brothers and sisters of the Bar/Bat Mitzvah.

Some would look upon these innovative prayers, prayer books and formats with disfavor. Personally, I find the attempt to update and keep our prayer services fresh and creative a very worthwhile, meaningful and healthy sign that Conservative Judaism is meeting the challenge of our times. As Israel Zangwill expressed it in *Dreamers of the Ghetto*, "Like a language, a religion is dead when it ceases to change." The liturgical revolution in American Judaism is a sign that we are alive and well.

11
Litany for the Yom Kippur War

(In Remembrance of the Yom Kippur War, 1973)

FOR THESE I WEEP —

My heart aches . . . .
For a Yom Kippur interrupted, and given to fighting and killing instead of to fasting and praying

My heart aches . . . .
For a time of quiet, six years of no war, shattered by blasphemy and treachery

My heart aches . . . .
For young boys and young men, whose strong bodies were massacred on their most solemn and sacred day of Judgment

My heart aches . . . .
For families broken, lives ended, children orphaned, parents bereaved, wives widowed

My heart aches . . . .
For strong hearts that have been stilled, open smiles that have been closed, for the waste of life - young, promising, and beautiful

Recited during Martyrology. Written by Arnold Turetsky and Dov Peretz Elkins.

My heart aches . . . .
 For the people of a young, new nation - just a quarter century old, that has become too old too soon - from the death of its young people

My heart aches . . . .
 For searing photos of Israeli prisoners, and burning Stars of David in the sky, for a Sefer Torah in captivity

My heart aches . . . .
 For hateful nations who applaud our enemies, who sit on the fence and pile guilt upon guilt to their already heavy burden

My heart aches . . . .
 For a Jewish Grandmother, born in Russia, reared in America, leader in Zion, whose reign and life were burdened with a new and heavy grief

My heart aches . . . .
 For God. Once again God was hidden, concealed behind the tragic convergence of violent lines. Is God angry, is God guilty, is God silent, is God? My hearts aches for you, God.

And my heart aches . . . .
 For me and my children. I want my children to believe that the world is good and that mankind is kind. But this is our world—violent and painful and something is wrong with mankind—and all we can do is pray, and give and commit ourselves. So we shall commit ourselves, and give, and we shall pray—if not to praise God then to seek Him.

PART II
Humanizing Religious Education

12
Humanistic Education for Jewish Religious Schools

Everyone is concerned about the rise in intermarriage, the onslaught of increasing assimilation, the corrosive acids of secularization, and the general drifting away from Jewish life by more and more of our young people.

Rabbi Max Routtenberg, a past president of the Rabbinical Assembly and leading figure in Conservative Judaism, has recently summarized his analysis of the state of Jewish schools: "After several decades of work with the congregational school, we declare unequivocally that we have achieved none of the limited goals that we have set, nor have we even approximated them. None of the thousands of children that have been put in our care learned to use Hebrew functionally, either for speaking or reading purposes; none learned to read the *humash* in Hebrew with the most elementary degree of understanding; none learned to read the Siddur with an understanding of the prayers. Yet, three-quarters of the time in class was devoted to these three major subjects. Even a modest measure of fluency in mechanical Siddur reading was never acquired by the majority of the children. As for the other subjects . . . Jewish history, religion, customs and ceremonies, current topics, music, administered in tiny

Published in *Religious Education,* March, 1976.

capsules, one needs little imagination to know how superficial and inconsequential the knowledge thus acquired."[1]

This evaluation is serious enough, but then Rabbi Routtenberg draws the following dismal conclusion from his appraisal:

> The most tragic consequence is not the wasted years and the lost opportunities, but the great distaste and the negative attitudes that have been generated in the children. And since these unhappy years have been spent under the roof of the synagogue, it is little wonder that the parents find it difficult to 'drag' their children to services or to interest them in synagogue activities during their teen-age years. [2]

As part of the analysis of the national problem facing Jewish education, let me further share with you the contents of a full page advertisement in a national Jewish newspaper dated recently: "If you're Jewish, chances are your grandchildren won't be. That's right. Plain and simple: an ever-increasing rate of intermarriage, assimilation, alienation from Judaism, and a lack of Jewish education is resulting in a decline of American Jewry. . . . Current trends indicate that in a matter of time there will be no American Jewry to speak of . . . Finish. No more . . . . A substantial number of today's Jewish population are being raised without any knowledge of their history, culture and traditions of the Jewish people. And their children, your grandchildren, will probably be brought up without any Jewish thought . . . . in essence, lost to the Jewish way of life. No Jewish faith. No Jewish culture. No Jewish beliefs. And no Jewish experiences . . . ."[3]

This advertisement was sponsored by the Board of Jewish Education of New York. It helps us understand that the

---

[1]Max J. Routtenberg, *Decades of Decision*, an appraisal of American Jewish Life. New York: Bloch, 1973, p. 36.

[2]*Ibid.*, pp. 36-7.

[3]*American Examiner - Jewish Week*, 9-14-74, p. 20.

problem is not just one of Jewish schools, but of Jewish survival. I hasten to add that this problem is not confined to Jewish education, but to all supplemental religious education in America. It seems that Christian Sunday Schools have the same kind of problem we do. A generation ago Alfred North Whitehead assessed the value of Christian education by saying, "The vitality of religion is shown by the way in which the religious spirit has survived the ordeal of religious education."[4] This view is shared by the youngster who told his minister, "The man who invented Sunday school must have hated kids."

To go one step further, I now want to share an evaluation of general education made by the late distinguished professor of psychology at Brandeis University, Abraham Maslow. "Our conventional education," wrote Maslow, "looks mighty sick. . . . If . . . you ask the question about the courses that you took in high school, 'How did my trigonometry course help me to become a better human being?' an echo answers, 'By gosh, it didn't!' My early music education was also not very successful, because it taught a child who had a very profound feeling for music and a great love for the piano *not* to learn it. I had a piano teacher who taught me in effect that music is something to stay away from. And I had to relearn music as an adult, all by myself."[5]

Thus, it seems that education in America as a whole, at least in the view of those whose opinions I have studied, has been a dismal failure. For Christian education or general education the failure is serious enough, but for Jews for whom education is one of the cardinal principles of our faith and is the very key to our survival, it is a tragedy! Louis Marshall long ago warned us that, "If we, the Jewish people, ever come to the stage where we fail to respond to the call of

[4]*The Christian Century*, 2-20-74, p. 204.

[5]A.H. Maslow, *The Farther Reaches of Human Nature*, N.Y.: The Viking Press, 1972, p. 170.

Jewish education, we will have done what our enemies never succeeded in doing . . . . We will have destroyed ourselves. We will have written our own death warrant."[6]

So, if American public and religious education have failed miserably, we Jews cannot take comfort in their sorrow. If America has devoted all of its energies to space exploration, scientific discovery, and technological advancement, to the sad neglect of its institutions of learning, then we Jews must set an example of righting that wrong and of re-ordering our priorities.

Carl Rogers assessed our failures in education as serious enough to doom our entire civilization. "When I realize," he said, "the incredible potential in the ordinary student, I want to try to release it. We are working hard to release the incredible energy in the atom and the nucleus of the atom. If we do not devote equal energy—yes, and equal money—to the release of the potential of the individual person then the enormous discrepancy between our level of physical energy resources and human energy resources will doom us to a deserved and universal destruction."[7]

NEW CONCEPTIONS IN EDUCATION

Having presented a brief but gloomy picture of where we stand, let me now turn to some new conceptions that are beginning to emerge in general education among some innovative and creative educators today. Such new conceptions and ideas offer us renewed hope for a better day ahead in Jewish education.

[6]*A Treasury of Modern Jewish Thoughts,* edited by Sidney Greenberg, N.J.: Yoseloff, 1970, p. 161.

[7]Carl R. Rogers, *Freedom to Learn,* Columbus, Ohio: Charles E. Merrill, 1969, p. 125.

Education today can be divided into two major parts. The first is the imparting of information, facts, and knowledge called cognitive learning. The second is the transmission of values, dealing with feelings, influencing behavior and character—or humanistic education—also referred to as affective, and sometimes as confluent education. The latter kind, humanistic education, has been defined as "the identification for specific educational concern of the nonintellective side of learning: the side having to do with emotions, feelings, interests, values and character."[8]

It seems to me that while mastery of subject matter is extremely important in Jewish education—and I want to emphasize that point—that a healthy balance between the cognitive and the value elements of education will go a long way towards solving many of our problems in Jewish education today. At the very least, it will set goals that are more in keeping with the Jewish way of life, and be better designed to perpetuate our many-faceted heritage and help preserve Jewish identity and commitment.

For Judaism is a religion of great emotion, of color, of feeling. It is also a religion of values, of philosophy, of attitudes, and above all of high moral behavioral standards. If we don't at least attempt to educate in that direction, we are not really teaching Judaism!!

One of the great Hasidic masters once said, "I do not visit Rabbi Dov Ber of Mezrich to hear Torah from him but to watch him tie his shoelace." In other words, the most important thing one can learn from a teacher is not the words in a book, but modes of behavior. Another Hasidic tale recounts that an avid student rushed to his master one day and shouted excitedly, "Rabbi, I went through the whole

[8]Stuart Miller, in *Human Teaching for Human Learning* by George Isaac Brown, N.Y.: Viking Press, 1971, p. xvi.

Torah this week!" Whereupon the Rabbi replied, "Yes, but how much of the Torah went through you?"

The ultimate goal in Jewish education must be not only learning enough Hebrew to read and understand the Torah, but to find a teacher who can help the student live Torah, become Torah, and accept the values and behaviors contained in the Torah!

This means that the teacher in the religious school classroom will be concerned about the students' emotional state as well as his memorization of prayers and vocabulary. The teacher will have to excite and enthuse the children to appreciate and to enjoy Jewish learning and Jewish living. That is precisely where we have fallen down to date! We have overemphasized book learning to the exclusion of affective or confluent education—namely, the concern for the nonintellective side of the student—his feelings, interests, values and character.

Rabbi Jack J. Cohen, formerly of New York and now Director of the Hillel Foundation at the Hebrew University of Jerusalem, and one of the most sensitive educators I know, wrote some years ago that ". . . the goal of all education should be the cultivation of better human beings . . . . Jewish educators must exhibit greater interest than heretofore in the personality and character growth of their students. . . . We give only lip-service to the idea that the religious school is meant to develop sensitive religious personalities . . . . "[9]

Professor Abraham Maslow, whom I quoted earlier, said this about the new, humanistic education: The chief concern of the overwhelming majority of teachers, principals, curriculum planners, school superintendents, is "with efficiency, that is, with implanting the greatest number of facts into the greatest possible number of children, with a minimum of

---

[9]*Jewish Education*, Vol. XXVI, No. 1, Summer, 1955. (Reprinted in *Judaism and the Jewish School.* N.Y.: Bloch, 1966, p. 313).

time, expense, and effort. On the other hand, there is the minority of humanistically oriented educators who have as their goal the creation of better human beings, or in psychological terms, self-actualization and self-transcendence."[10]

One of the great Jewish educators of our day, the late Philip Arian, who served in Albany and later as Director of the Bureau of Jewish Education in Chicago, believed deeply in the joy of Jewish living, and in transmitting the feeling and excitement of Jewish life. In a collection of his writings that I read recently, I found the following profound statement: "The goal of molding a student who loves the pursuit of knowledge for its own sake, who finds fulfillment in the act of study, whose love of books is continually whetted by abiding curiosity—even this exalted goal is insufficient. For we are not striving for a detached dilettantism, study for self amusement, or the molding of scholastic dabblers. Judaism bids us learn *al menat la-asot*, so that learning may lead to action. Action reflecting Judaism's ethical and ritual commandments, to strive for moral perfection, to reach up to the challenge destiny has decreed for us as a Kingdom of Priests, action reflecting a world desperately needing the Jewish concept of free men living by law—a world sorely needing Jewish sensitivity to the debilitated, the deprived, the dominated."[11]

Long, long ago, the ancient rabbis understood this humanistic goal of education when they laid out in the *ahava rabba* prayer, before the Shma, their conception of goal-setting in life, *lilmod ule-lamed, lishmor ve-laasot ulekayem*—"to learn, to teach, to observe, to do, and to fulfill all the words of instruction in Thy Torah." Not just to learn, but to

[10]Op Cit. chapter 13, "The Goals and Implications of Humanistic Education." pp. 180-1. Cf. also George B. Leonard, *Education and Ecstasy*. N.Y.: Dell. 1968. "What is Education?" pp. 1-21.

[11]Speech to the Albany Hebrew Academy, November 20, 1966.

do, to fulfill! *Laasot ulekayem*! We must deal in education with the whole person, his mind, his heart, his body, and not just his capacity to memorize facts.

In the new kind of education, the arts will have an extremely important role. Music, dance, drawing, drama, ritual and pagentry will all be meaningful experiences of prayer. Not just rote recitation, but significant transcendent acts of public worship, in the class, in the sanctuary, and even outdoors whenever possible.

It is widely agreed that one of the most successful enterprises in Jewish education today is Camp Ramah. In the environment and atmosphere of total Jewish living, where the Shabbat is experienced and not just talked about, and where song and prayer and dance and joy are lived in a beautiful outdoor setting, where the presence of God is felt most intensely, the child *feels* Judaism and not just hears about Judaism. This is humanistic education at its best.

But not every child can go to Ramah, and even if that were possible, a summer camp experience covers only one-sixth of the year. What about the majority of our children who cannot get to Ramah, and the other ten months for those who do? It is my firm conviction that ways can be found to bring the Ramah atmosphere, the humanistic approach, into the winter months, and into the religious school, and into the life of the congregation.

In my congregation, we have already begun to do this with our Havurah and Mishpacha groups. In these small groups, emotion is felt and people are enjoyed for the love and warmth and support they offer. Learning takes place in an atmosphere that is warm, accepting, and stimulating. There are many more ways of emphasizing education for values, for character, for the emotions. These include total family programs and discussions, family life education, parent education, and weekend retreats, among other things. Anyone who has spent a weekend at a camp setting, in an intensive Jewish atmosphere, knows that Jewish education can be fun. inspiring, and exciting and at the same time enlightening, intellectually stimulating, and nourishing.

THE NEED FOR CHARACTER EDUCATION WITHIN AND OUTSIDE THE CLASSROOM

The new concept means expanding education outside the classroom, and making much greater use of informal settings, of weekends away, of summers, of the youth program, of total family activities, for motivating our students to see the joy of Jewish learning and Jewish living. We may need to re-organize our congregational administrative structures to replace the several different committees which now operate our school, youth program, adult education, and family activities into one broad commision on congregational education, with sub-committees for the various branches of education. To see them as unrelated departments and to have them operate totally independently is to miss the supreme opportunity that a congregational setting for education offers. We are modeling our structure after the public schools and we shouldn't. We need our own unique structure to integrate the learning of all our members, young and old, in the classroom and outside, winter and summer, cognitive and affective learning, in the home, the school, and away at retreat centers.

It is not the structure, of course, but the end product that counts. And the end product must be a Jewish family, not just a child, that grows Jewishly every day; that learns together; that discusses Jewish issues at the dinner table; that prepares together as well as separately for the coming of Shabbat and holidays; that is proud of being Jewish because Judaism adds a new dimension to their lives, to their family, to their congregation, and to their community. They will be a family that thrills to own and study Jewish books, and that is open to sharing their feelings about what they find in the books; that lives out the ethical imperatives in the book, that works together as well as individually for the betterment of the general community as well as for the Jewish community, for our world today is merely one global village and human freedom and dignity is a seamless web; a family whose vision is as broad as humanity and as profound as 4000 years of Jewish history.

I believe that we can have this kind of education in American Judaism. It is a new and different conception, even though its roots go as far back as the ancient rabbis and the Bible before them. It is a vision of a living and vibrant Jewish community responding to the challenges of the 1970s and the 1980s, not afraid to grow and change, because nothing is frightening or forbidding when the education of our children and ourselves is at stake, and when the future survival of Judaism may very well be in jeopardy!

If we can create this kind of total learning community, where love and concern are the primary goals of education, and where the joy of mastering knowledge inspires and enlightens together, then we are on the first rung of the ladder reaching toward a society of authenticity, of justice, of community, and of happiness, and peace. We must never be afraid to dream in broad strokes and to reach higher than we think we can grasp.

13
The Joy of Jewish Learning

In the previous essay I wrote of a new kind of education that is slowly spreading across America: humanistic education, which has as its goal the education of the heart as well as of the mind; education for life and character, for behaving and feeling, as well as for knowing.

One of the assumptions in this kind of education is that a person's character, his sensitivity, his emotional life is as important, if not more important, than his intellectual life. This new wave reflects to some degree an old Talmudic debate which raged in the academies of Babylonia 2000 years ago, between those who argued that deeds are more important than study, and those who said that study is more important than deeds. The resolution of the conflict was that study which led to the performance of good deeds was the best of both worlds.[1]

In this essay I want to concentrate on one significant aspect of the life of the emotions that I consider central not only to successful education, but to all of life. I refer to the sense of joy and enthusiasm which is so vital and indispensable

Published in *Religious Education,* March, 1976.
[1]Talmud, Kiddushin 40b.

an ingredient in the classroom and in all of life. To have successful education, learning must be filled with joy and excitement. To have a satisfying life, one must find opportunities to be happy and joyous.

In the *musaf* prayer of the Days of Awe, we have a graphic picture of how the ancient rabbis envisioned the Messianic age which can be considered their idealized vision of man and society. "Uv-chen tzadikkim yiru ve-yismacha, veesharim ya-alozu, va-hasidim be-rina yagilu . . . ." "Then shall the righteous rejoice, the upright exult in triumph, and the pious celebrate in song . . . ."[2]

Going back even further into our religious history, the biblical Book of Psalms is replete with a sense of joy, excitement, and enthusiasm about life and the beauty and thrill of living in the world God created. In Psalm 100, to pick merely one example of scores of passages, we read: "Acclaim the Lord, all the earth! Serve the Lord with gladness. Come before Him with joyous song."

Two years ago, the late Mark Van Doren, distinguished poet, critic, and author, addressed an audience of Jewish students in a talk called, interestingly enough for a non-Jew, "Le-chayim, to life".[3] Professor Van Doren said: "Happiness is when you feel good and don't know why. It isn't anything planned, it isn't how you ever thought your ought to feel. You simply do, and God help you if this never happens in your life. It happens only to strong people; for it takes strength to be happy." Then, after quoting several verses from the Bible about joy and happiness, Van Doren concludes with a quotation from the Book of Proverbs and some comments on them.

---

[2] *The High Holyday Prayer Book*, ed. B.Z. Bokser (N.Y.: Hebrew Publishing Co., 1969), p. 175.

[3] *Keeping Posted*, Vol. XVII, No. 8, May, 1972, pp. 3ff.

A merry heart maketh a cheerful countenance;
But by sorrow of heart the spirit is broken.
All the days of the poor are evil;
But he that is of a merry heart hath a continual feast.

"Was this making the best of a bad bargain?" asked Van Doren. He then proceeded to answer his own question: "I rather think it was saying that life, even in the most terrible conceivable times, is the best bargain. It is what can be said now, when the future of the world, if there is any such thing, is thought to be blacker than ever before. It can be said, but only by powerful and passionate souls, by persons who can bear the enormous burden of joy that still descends on those who have been chosen to receive it. Hallelujah."[4]

Another modern non-Jewish thinker captured this same ancient Jewish viewpoint. I refer to Eric Hoffer, who said, "On the whole, it seems to be true that the creative periods in history were buoyant and even frivolous. . . .One suspects that much of the praise of seriousness comes from people who have a vital need for a facade of weight and dignity. La Rochefoucauld said of solemnity that it is a 'mystery of the body invented to conceal the defects of the mind. '"[5]

Whoever saw the play or motion picture, "Fiddler on the Roof,"—and who didn't—will testify to the joy in the heart of Tevya, the simple milkman, who lived in an age that was difficult for all men, let alone Jews, and who never knew if he would have enough bread to feed his family for another day. Tevya took such great pleasure in life—he sang, he danced, he jumped, he studied, he quoted or misquoted the Scriptures, he took pride and pleasure in being a son of God, a Jew, a human being.

[4]*Ibid.,* p. 5.
[5]Quoted in George B. Leonard, *Education and Ecstasy,* (N.Y.: Delta, 1968), p. 99.

JOY THROUGH MITZVOT

This leads me to the point that it is the carrying out of the customs, ceremonies, laws, traditions, mandates, of Judaism that can bring some of the greatest experiences of joy and excitement to man.

Some of our Christian theologians today are finding the Jewish spirit of joy to be an increasingly more important aspect of their religious life. Dr. Howard J. Clinebell, a distinguished minister and professor, wrote recently: "One form of enjoyment that is often neglected is religious enjoyment—the uplifting, numinous, and ecstatic elements in religious experience. The spine-tingling qualities in vital religion are often missing in conventional churches. In Jungian terms, the masculine elements in religion (reason, logic, ethics, controls) are present without the balancing feminine elements (feeling, giving, accepting, nurturing). This accounts, in part, for the popularity of the sect groups which encourage their adherents to feel and enjoy their religion."[6]

Life without joy is not life in its fullest sense. Furthermore, religion and religious education are forces that should foster a sense of joy and enthusiasm in our daily lives. We have many burdens in our years on earth: sickness, suffering, death of dear ones; problems of economics, of war and peace, of personal relationships, of anger and conflict. Religion must help us maintain a balanced and wholesome view of it all or we will surely buckle under these burdens.

It is interesting that the very word "enthusiasm" has the word God within it. The middle syllable, "t h u s" is from the Greek word "theos", meaning God. Enthusiasm means a spirit touched by divine ardor, by the spirit of joy and

[6]*Mental Health Through Christian Community,* (Nashville: Abingdon, 1965), p. 38.

happiness which God represents. It is that spirit of enthusiasm which we must recapture in our lives and transmit to our children in and out of our classrooms, for without it life would be unbearable!

The story is told of a watchman who was called to testify after the collision of two ships at sea. He was asked whether or not he was standing on the dock holding the lantern. He answered in the affirmative. After he stepped down, he seemed nervous and tense. He was asked to explain this nervousness; since he was holding the lantern, what would there be to be unhappy about? "I was afraid they would ask me if the lantern were lit." That is the question for us. We stand on the dock of life, holding the lantern, the guideposts for us and our children, but is it lit? Is there that crucial light of enthusiasm, of joy, of excitement?

The late Rabbi Heschel often told a favorite story of his about a young man who wanted to become a blacksmith. He apprenticed to an experienced blacksmith and learned all the techniques of the trade—how to hold the tongs, to lift the sledge, to smite the anvil, and even how to blow the fire with the bellows. After finishing his apprenticeship, he was chosen to be the smith at the royal palace. But his delight was soon ended when he discovered that while he learned all the other techniques, he had failed to learn how to kindle a spark. All the other skills and techniques were meaningless without that essential spark.[7]

No group illustrates this approach to life better than the Hasidic movement in Judaism during the past two centuries. To the Hasidic way of thinking, melancholy is a barrier to the service and worship of the Almighty. The ideal of *hitlahavut,* or religious fervor, was crucial to everything the Hasid did. Rabbi Menachem Mendel of Vitebsk said to his disciples: Rejoice that you have an opportunity to sing about God.

[7]*Women's League Outlook*, Summer, 1973.

Rejoice that you are a Jew. Rejoice for you are able to pray, to study and perform God's will.[8]

JOY IN WORSHIP

It is my belief that the *hitlahavut,* the religious fervor, of Hasidic Judaism, is a sorely missing ingredient in the life of the American synagogue, in its religious services, in its schoolrooms, in its programs, and throughout the institution. Let me illustrate this point with a story about a church in New York that reminds me of many American synagogues. It was a large, formal, high ceilinged building with ushers marching up and down the aisles, from time to time, telling people to sit still and be quiet during the worship. At this particular church, a black woman from the South was in attendance who hailed from a totally different kind of religious environment, where noise and joy were the expected norm. During the minister's sermon she kept yelling out, "Amen - Amen!" An usher scurried over and asked if she were ill. "Ill?", she replied, "Absolutely not. I got religion." "Please," answered the solicitous usher, "not in here!"

That is what I am afraid is happening to the American synagogue. We are missing the *hitlahavut* of the old traditional shtiebel, where singing, dancing, yelling, and joyous enthusiasm were an integral part of Jewish worship. "Not in here!"

Our religious services in America are modelled after the Protestant worship of 18th century Europe, where decorum and silence were the rule. When Reform Judaism was born in the early 19th century in Germany, the synagogue was Germanized and Protestantized, and we have not yet learned that it must be re-Judaized and Hasidized. In 1838, in a synagogue in Wuerttemberg, a number of rules were passed

[8] *Keeping Posted* (cf. note 3), p. 8.

by the congregational leadership, to insure the new spirit of decorum and dignity of the age. I quote them to you:

The synagogue should be entered with decorum and without noise. He who enters must immediately go to his seat and remain in it as quietly as possible. . . . . Any walking around or standing together within the synagogue is prohibited on pain of punishment . . . . as being offensive to the decorum and to the dignity of the worship service, the practice of the following customs is no longer permitted in the synagogue: (a) kissing of the curtain on entering the synagogue or during the service; (b) leaving one's seat in order to kiss the Scroll of the Law; (c) knocking during the reading of the Book of Esther on the feast of Purim; (d) the malkoth-beating on the eve of the Day of Atonement; (e) the noisy beating of hosanoth on the 7th day of Tabernacles; (f) sitting on the floor on the fast of the Ninth of Ab; (g) removing shoes and boots in the synagogue on that day; (h) the procession with the Torah which is still the practice in some localities on the eve of Rejoicing in the Law; (i) the procession of the children with flags and candles on that festival; (j) the distribution of food and drink in the synagogue on that festival in localities where it is still taking place. [9]

If I were to look for a program of things to restore to the synagogue today, the first thing I would do would be to check that list and see how many of the customs listed we have not already restored, and try to restore almost every one of them. (I would probably omit the beatings on the eve of Yom Kippur.)

Mr. Philip Arian, the Jewish educator whom I quoted before, wrote the following in *Response* magazine: "We Jews

---

[9]"Reform Judaism: Evolution and the Stork," by Norman Mirsky, *Judaism*, Vol. 23, Summer 1974, p. 309.

are uptight and joyless. Sometimes we dance and sing, but our heads are in the way. Often the spark flames dangerously close to the surface but we are afraid to give in to the uninhibited Jewishness we suspect is ready to erupt. I have captured this spark and make it serve me. I feel mine is a boundless, bubbling, irrepressible kind of Jewishness . . . ." [10]

This is the approach I think we need more of in our religious school classrooms in the American synagogue. It is in keeping with the ideas of the humanistic educators I referred to above, but really is an old Jewish notion that life is good, that joy is indispensable in all living, and especially in learning.

The famous 18th century scholar Elijah the Vilna Gaon was once asked, if an angel were to reveal to him all the knowledge of the Torah that was possible to know, would he be content to stop studying the sacred books? His answer was: Absolutely not! He would be very sad, in fact, because that would deprive him of one of the greatest joys in life that he knows: the joy of learning something new.

JOY IN EDUCATION

In an article in a recent issue of *Saturday Review/World* (8-24-74), Harold Howe, former U.S. Commissioner of Education, prognosticates about what education will be like in the year 2024, 50 years from now. Mr. Howe's article is written from the perspective of the year 2024, as if he were looking back on the half-century between 1974 and 2024. After describing what the new directions of education looked like in those years, he writes: "The overall effect of this mode and style of education has been to change its atmosphere

[10]Quoted in a mimeographed collection of Arian's writings.

completely. While there are still those who hold to the bitter-pill theory of learning—that the more unpleasant it is, the better it is for you—they are now in retreat. In many schools and colleges, education is fun and at the same time successful. It is gradually fulfilling the hopes of a futurist who wrote in 1967: 'People will increasingly demand the right to study and learn because it will be a source of great satisfaction.' But he qualified this with the observation that 'it may be impossible for us to accept the idea that learning can be enjoyable, that it should not entail frustration and boredom, punishment or failure, dread, shame, or panic! None of this implies, incidentally, that concentration and effort are not important components of the new emphasis in many schools and colleges. They are important and accepted elements of learning.'"[11]

Professor Abraham Maslow, the humanistic psychologist whom I quoted above, also related joy to the learning experience, when he said: "One of the goals of education should be to teach that life is precious. If there were no joy in life, it would not be worth living. Unfortunately many people never experience joy, those all-too-few moments of total life affirmation which we call peak experiences. . . .We know that children are capable of peak experiences and that they happen frequently during childhood. We also know that the present school system is an extremely effective instrument for crushing peak experiences and forbidding their possibility. The natural child-respecting teacher who is not frightened by the sight of children enjoying themselves is a rare sight in classrooms. . . . Even the difficult tasks of learning to read and subtract and multiply, which are necessary in an industrialized society, can be enhanced and made joyful."[12]

[11] Pages 73-4.

[12] "Goals and Implications of Humanistic Education," in *The Farther Reaches of Human Nature* (N.Y.: Viking, 1971), pp. 187-8.

A very popular account of humanistic education that was on the best seller lists a few years ago is *Education and Ecstasy,* by George B. Leonard, who shares Maslow's views on the joys of learning. Leonard points out that many great scholars and artists throughout history have greeted their moments of learning with ecstatic joy. "We learn," he writes, "how Archimedes leaped, crying 'Eureka!' from his bathtub; how Handel, on finishing the 'Hallelujah Chorus,' told his servant, 'I did think I did see all Heaven before me, and the great God himself'; how Nietzsche wrote *Thus Spake Zarathustra:* (by saying)

> There is an ecstasy such that the immense strain
> of it is sometimes relaxed by a flood of tears . . . .

What we fail to acknowledge," Leonard concludes, "is that every child starts out as an Archimedes, a Handel, a Nietzsche. . . . To follow ecstasy in learning - in spite of injustice, suffering, confusion and disappointment - is to move more easily toward an education, a society that would free the enormous potential of man."[13]

No, our schools cannot perform miracles, but they can work together with the home, the community, and the synagogue to foster an education geared toward the mind and the heart, the brain and the emotions, the intellect and character, knowledge and behavior.

All of us can find more zest and more enthusiasm in our lives. We can renew ourselves, renew our lives by deciding that we will seek joy, excitement and enthusiasm in those things which we value most, such as religious observance, being with friends, serving the community, reading a book, or whatever worthwhile activity "turns you on."

[13] George B. Leonard, *Education and Ecstasy* (N.Y.: Viking, 1968), pp. 232-4. See all of Chapter 13, "The Uses of Ecstasy."

We can begin to teach our children that life is too precious to waste on prolonged and over-indulging sorrow and melancholy, and on a surfeit of seriousness.

Let a spirit of religious fervor enter our homes, our schools, and our personal lives. Let the Sabbath be a time for exuberance and let the festivals be occasions for joy as the prayer says: *moadim le-simcha.* Let our lives revolve around the great simchas which life brings us, a bris, a baby-naming, a bar or bat mitzvah, a wedding, an anniversary, a new book read, a new chapter studied, a new ritual learned, a new friend made.

Put away sorrow and sighing and reach into your natural talent for laughter and jumping and singing and hugging. We all have it within us to be happy people, to be grateful for a world of beauty and goodness, and for the privileges of serving man and God.

If any people in the world has a right to be cynical and vengeful because of injustice and persecution, it is the Jewish people. And yet, despite all the centuries of wandering and exile and poverty and anti-Semitism, we are the people whose philosophy is expressed in a simple Hebrew phrase which has become universal. It is this phrase and this attitude that goes along with it that must begin again to permeate our lives, our homes, and our classrooms: Le-Chaim! To Life!

14
Humanizing Preaching

HUMANISTIC PSYCHOLOGY

I am presently completing a doctoral degree (Doctor of Ministry, D.Min. for short) at Colgate Rochester Divinity School, with a concentration in counseling and human relations training. The area of learning in which I have been most heavily involved is humanistic psychology. Humanistic psychology is the so-called "third force" of psychology, following Freudian analysis and behaviorism. Humanistic psychology, first identified and profoundly influenced by Abraham H. Maslow, the late Brandeis professor, builds upon psychoanalysis, and behaviorism but goes beyond it. It believes there is more to persons than sexual urges, childhood influences and environmental control. It takes heavily into account personal responsibility, fulfillment of human potential, creativity, joy, ecstasy, self-transcendence, and other "spiritual factors." It is closer to Judaism and religion in general than the other psychological schools which tend to denigrate religion. In fact, in close concert with religious approaches, it stresses the personal, moral, and altruistic

Published in *Beineinu,* The Journal of the Rabbinical Assembly, October, 1975.

forces at work within a human being as a unique and sacred creature. Its themes are remarkably close to the issues with which religion has dealt for the past four thousand years.

MY OWN PREACHING

Truth to tell, finding sermon themes has not been an easy task for me in my eleven years in the rabbinate. Especially in the first six years, I was heavily dependent upon the work of other men, such as Israel Levinthal, Sidney Greenberg, Saul Teplitz, etc. The sermon volumes I myself published (*So Young to Be a Rabbi*, 1969; *A Tradition Reborn*, 1973) concentrated on themes on which I felt most strongly: social action, Zionism, Soviet Jewry. There is a marked absence of sermons in these two volumes, and in my other published writings, of themes which deal with the sticky issues of life: personal effectiveness; personal growth; love and intimacy; individuality; happiness; responsibility; grief; celebration; etc., etc. For such themes I relied heavily on the work of many colleagues and sermon manuals. It has been uncomfortable for me and others' words never came easily out of my mouth - but they came nonetheless.

Within the past five or six years, I have changed my preaching style and themes selected, as I became more and more familiar with the writings of Eric Fromm, Carl Rogers, Rollo May, Viktor Frankl and others. These psychologists/ teachers are part of the burgeoning movement of humanistic psychology which for many is a substitute religion in secular America. Since my personal commitment is strongly to traditional Judaism (freely interpreted), I did not throw the baby out with the bath water, but rather read the works of these men in the light of Judaism. It became more and more apparent as years passed that their vocabulary, content, and searching was a religious one. The self-actualizing person, the ideal of humanistic psychology, is in my scheme the man of faith, the shutaf b'maasay breshit—God's partner in the ongoing creation of the world—the fulfiller of God-given human potential. The framework of humanistic psychology, the inspiration of the writers who explicated its themes, have given me new directions, exciting sermon themes, and a vehicle to see life whole and steady, and a mechanism with which to interpret and experience life.

A FEW EXAMPLES

When I discovered that the Bible deals with the spiritual struggle of man to find meaning, truth, joy, and fulfillment in the world, my preaching opened up and flowed naturally out of my new philosophy and psychology. I began to look at the people of the Bible, their struggles, their problems, their inadequacies, their failures, their searching and their exhilarations, as the stuff of my own life and that of my parishioners, my listeners, my charges. When I reached that point, I became a preacher instead of a parrot.

When I began to see clearly and sharply that the things that bind people of the past and people of today are essentially the few irreducible issues of the painful struggle to wrest meaning out of life, my words began to be filled with spontaneity, authenticity, and excitement. Humanistic psychology has given me a handle on life, and, hence, on preaching. The heartiest recommendation I can give to a preacher is to find a way to understand, appreciate, and grapple with life and share that struggle with your listeners/students.

Now when I preach, I use Joseph as an example of sibling rivalry, Korach as an example of personal and social conflict,

Elijah as an example of passionate radicalism, Jacob as an example of a stricken conscience, Jonah as a person struggling inadequately for fulfillment, and Ruth as a searcher for meaning. I can more easily relate the lives of these people and the incidents in thier biographies to what is happening to me and my congregants. It sounds unbelievably simple. Yet, simple as it may be, it has not been for me an easy path to uncover.

In addition to the biblical biographies, the laws, mythologies, legends, historical narratives, and rabbinic embellishments of the above, are all ready grist for the preacher's mill. I use humanistic psychology to carry me from the biblical and rabbinic ground to the superstructure of understanding the forces that operate in human life to promote growth, meaning, creativity, and fulfillment. For me, it has been an endless mine of new insights, inspiration, direction and challenge.

RESOURCES

Appended is a list of some of the themes discussed in books on humanistic psychology, which, as the reader will readily see, are the themes of the Bible, of religion, and more importantly, of human life. Also appended is a list of books which amplify the themes listed and in which the reader will find a rich and fruitful source of sermonic ideas.

Somewhat hesitantly and with some modesty, I would like to offer to speak to any group of colleagues, or boards of rabbis, on some of the exciting themes that have presented themselves to me as a result of my work in humanistic psychology during the past several years. I make this offer at the present, for the year 5736, with no expectation of remuneration.

THEMES IN HUMANISTIC PSYCHOLOGY

Love	Work
Sex	Relationship
Creativity	Conflict
Intimacy	Transcendence
Self-Concept	Joy
The nature of man	Feelings
Mind and body	Personal Growth
Role models	Authenticity, truth
Guilt	Intuition
Wholeness (Shalom)	Higher consciousness
Spirituality	Full humanness
Ecstasy	Risk
Responsibility	Fulfillment
Meaning	Life energy
Will	Self-confidence
Celebration	Self-esteem
Communication	Dignity
Individuality	Human potential
Family	Parenting
Values	Power
Good and evil	Masks
Autonomy	Maturity
Peak experience	Compassion
Courage	Humor
Spontaneity	Altruism
Intensity	

15
An Experiential Learning Model on Interdating

THE THEME OF INTERDATING

During the past nearly two decades of working closely with pre-teens and teenagers, I have come to recognize that the issue of interdating is one of the most value-laden and confusion-filled for young people. In homes where Judaism is of little import, where there is little manifest concern for Jewish culture or even ultimate Jewish survival, the issue of dating and marrying out of the faith is still a live and burning question.

Not only is the issue of interdating one of great perplexity and confusion for young Jewish people and their families, but that problem in turn leads to increasing difficulty in family communication. When children and parents experience barriers in relating over this crucial issue, they tend to begin to become polarized over other related and unrelated issues, which further advances the generation gap.

Thus, I felt it an area of value clarification which needed a new approach, a different method than traditional discussion techniques utilized in teenage youth groups and class-

Published in *Jewish Education,* Fall, 1975.

rooms. Out of my studies in humanistic education and human relations training came the idea to develop an experiential learning model on the issue of interdating.

EXPERIENTIAL LEARNING

The new methods developed in the field of humanistic education have placed great stress on experiential learning as opposed to the traditional form of lecture-discussion. Through using a structured experience, such as a game, a role-play, a simulation, or other motivating and involving activity, participants gain insight into a problem that would not come from merely hearing about it from an expert. Participants gain knowledge both through active participation in the structured experience, as well as sharing reactions, generalizations and applications from themselves and other group members. The teacher facilitates this process, but does not create it in the sense of giving a lecture or speech.

THE INTERDATING MODEL

The writer experimented with an experiential learning model on interdating recently that produced excellent results. Rather than lecturing the students on the pitfalls of interdating, the problems of assimilation, high divorce rates, identity-less children, etc., etc., an experiential model was designed and carried out, a description of which follows. The goals of the model were:

1. Exposure to viewpoints of others on the issue of interdating
2. Intergenerational communication and dialogue on interdating

3. Existential experiencing of viewpoints and feelings of those having ideas opposed to one's own
4. Avoidance of hostile confrontations between teenagers and parents, and of unproductive debates and resulting negative feelings.

INTRODUCTION

Members of the synagogue's LTF group (Leaders Training Fellowship) that meets monthly in my home, were invited to bring their parents to the last meeting of the year, in June, 1975. Approximately fifteen teenagers and thirty parents attended.

It was a beautiful Shabbat afternoon and folding chairs were set up on the lawn alongside the house. The group of forty-five participants met first in one large circle for introductory comments. I explained that the usual kind of parent-teenage discussion in interdating usually turns into a free-for-all brawl, with no one agreeing and only hostility resulting. I stated my position on the issue clearly by saying that I considered interdating to be potentially dangerous. I also said that I believe in the ultimate responsibility of each person to make his own life's decisions. It was my surmise, I explained, that the teenagers probably agreed with me on the second point and the parents on the first.

Since there were apt to be some many disagreements and strong feeling on these issues, it was unlikely that any conclusions would be achieved or anyone's mind changed easily. My goals, therefore, were not to have a debate or to reach any pat answers, but to share viewpoints, attitudes, and feelings. If only we could come away after the two hour meeting with a better understanding of the viewpoint of another person, especially the viewpoint of another generation, the time would have been spent worthily.

THE ROLE-PLAY

New knowledge from the field of group dynamics tells us that in a passionately argued issue such as interdating, an effective method of dialogue is to have each person argue from the viewpoint of the person holding an opposing viewpoint. I thus asked the group to divide into groups of three, with two adults and one teenager in each triad, the only stipulation being that no two people in any triad be from one family. Thus, the two adults could not be spouses and the teenager could not be the child of either of them. There was one adult male, one adult female, and one teenager in each group. The teenager was to take the role of the parent and the two adults the role of two teenage children in the family. The warmth and trust built up in the LTF group during the year was enough to extend into the entire adult-teenage group and enable the role-play to succeed. While a few people later commented that the role-play was too brief and artificial, most of the participants felt it was effective enough to derive significant learnings.

Instructions were to have the "parent" try to persuade the two "teenagers" not to interdate. The "teenagers" were to argue back, marshalling as many cogent theses for their side as possible, namely, that interdating was "o.k." They were told they would have about ten minutes, which turned out to be close to fifteen, since they looked very animated during the dialoguing. I cut off the discussion while it still looked vigorous and before it might become tedious. The role-playing dialogue permitted all of the important arguments to emerge without creating lasting tensions between adults and teenagers. It also enabled participants to see the issue from the viewpoint of the opposite side.

PROCESSING

The entire group gathered together to process their experience. The first step was to get out the information produced by the role-play. For ten minutes the participants surfaced all the arguments brought out by both sides for and against interdating. Each person quoted himself or another participant, in a summarizing way, so that the entire dialogue was not re-created. No one repeated an argument already stated and no one was permitted to refute any argument, only to mention it and lay it on the table.

The next step, also about ten minutes in length, was to have each participant, who wanted to do so, relate his experience of taking a viewpoint he disagreed with and of hearing his own viewpoint from someone whom he would ordinarily expect to espouse the other stance. In other words, what learnings were there from experiencing this role-play? Several participants felt that they understood both sides of the question more clearly and were able to empathize much better with their children (or parents). Both generations seemed to have attained new insights into the other generation's feelings and attitudes.

As I walked around from group to group during the role-play, it became obvious that both parents and teenagers were actively absorbed in their roles. Young people warned their "children" that the first step of interdating would lead eventually to intermarriage. Parents, in turn, pleaded (in the role of teenagers) that unless they dated non-Jews their circle of friends would be severely restricted. This, they claimed, was patently unfair. Had they not been taught to respect all peoples, regardless of color or creed? How could their "parents" now tell them to avoid Gentiles in dating relationships? The teenage/parents defended their position vociferously. It was acceptable and even commendable to be friends with a Gentile, but dates were of another order. How could they perpetuate Judaism if they ultimately ended up in an intermarriage?

It became obvious after watching several of the small groups that this experiential empathizing was having a strong effect. This observation was later confirmed when the participants reported that their understanding of their parents/children grew immeasurably from taking their side in the debate.

Were I to utilize this model again, I would add an additional step in the processing at this point. I would ask parents to relate some of their feelings to the teenagers about their emotional reactions to the vision of their child's intermarrying. I would also invite the teenagers to express their feelings about the possibility of their parents' violently rejecting them should they intermarry. Some of these views came out of the discussion, but this would create a natural opportunity to insure that each person had a chance to share this and to have the entire group consider the depth of these feelings.

It should be noted that no one at any time was embarrassed into speaking. Everyone was free to talk at any juncture, as long as it was not interrupting another speaker, and it was on the topic and not an unhelpful digression. I reflected the content and feelings of the speakers as a reinforcing device, but did not evaluate the comments, positively or negatively, of any speaker. This encouraged maximum participation.

The learning that emerged most strongly from the teenage group revolved around the issue of Jewish survival. These were youngsters who have been attending Hebrew High School, some of them frequenting Hebrew culture camps in the summer, and who have a stronger commitment to Jewish life than the average young Jew. What seemed to appeal to their survivalist instincts most was the idea that the Jewish people and the Jewish heritage could not be maintained in a situation of widespread intermarriage. (It would be interesting to compare the reaction should this model be repeated with less committed youngsters. My hypothesis is that since the gap would be greater than with committed youngsters, the learning would be even richer.)

Another important theme that surfaced strongly during the processing of the experiential model was that parents had to set an example of Jewish commitment before they had a right to demand avoidance of interdating from their children. Children would not accept a request to refrain from inter-dating without a strong demonstration from their parents that the ultimate objective of creative Jewish survival was an important desideratum to the parents. This commitment would have to be manifest in more ways than merely demanding that their children marry "nice Jewish spouses."

The final step in the processing was to ask the parents to state in one sentence any final attitude, feeling, or viewpoint they wanted to leave with the teenage group. Again, no refutations were permitted since such feelings and viewpoints were the property of the individuals and they were entitled to express them freely and without fear of refutation. It was to be an expression of one's learnings from the afternoon and a kind of summary of one's position—not a starting point for a debate. This activity was designed to give closure to the exchange. Renewal of the debate would surely have achieved only the opposite. The teenagers were then given their chance to state in one sentence any final statements they wished to leave with the parent community without response, positive or negative.

The summation statements were all made on the unspoken assumption that interdating was a dysfunctional behavior for those who believed in the welfare of the Jewish people. It was not a question of should one interdate, but how can we persuade more people to become more committed Jews. Young people again urged parents to demonstrate more live involvement in Jewish life, and parents enunciated again their hopes that their children would understand the need to balance an integrated life in American society with the preservation of a distinct sense of Jewish communality.

We concluded, as we do at every LTF meeting, with a friendship circle, each person crossing hands and joining with those to his left and right and singing Shalom Haverim.

All participants felt that the entire learning model was valuable for them and that they came away from the meeting with new understandings and insights, both cognitive and attitudinal. The goals were effectively achieved.

For facilitators of Jewish youth groups who might wish to replicate this model, careful attention should be given to setting the tone for the role-play (an atmosphere of group trust must be present for it to be effective); division into small groups should be done with expedition yet with care that family members are separated and that a good balance is made between parents and teenagers; ample time should be given to report out the data of the discussion (without becoming repetitious or boring), and to generalize some significant learnings that emerged from it; and finally, the group leader should not put him/herself in the position of arguing or moralizing - learning should flow from the group experience, be it positive or negative. The assumption is that in any given group of Jewish group members enough positive experiences will emerge to give the total program the emphasis desired by Jewish survivalists. If these directions come mostly from the teacher/facilitator, then the whole purpose of the experiential learning is lost. One might as well have just given a lecture. When commiting ourselves to the experiential modality, we must be prepared to accept the learnings that emerge from the experience, and hope that, if careful preparation and execution is achieved, the learnings will be beneficial, as they were in this case.

16
Some Materials for Humanizing the Bar/Bat Mitzvah

THOUGHT PROVOKER FOR BAR/BAT MITZVAH CANDIDATES
HOW I FEEL ABOUT . . .

Note: Please fill out and bring with you to your discussion with Rabbi Elkins. Be as brief or lengthy as you wish. Please be honest and open. There are no right answers and therefore whatever you think is right for you. Think about the question and your answer before writing. However, don't "edit" your answers in accord with what you think the Rabbi wants to hear. Your answers will be the basis for discussion. You will not be marked or criticized in any way for what you write.

1. My Haftara means to me_____

_____

_____

2. I want to be Bar/Bat Mitzvah because _____

_____

_____

3. I like being Jewish because _____

4. The most important think I learned this year in Religious School is _____

5. I dream that _____

THOUGHT CATALYST FOR BAR/BAT MITZVAH PARENTS

What Does Judaism Mean To Me?

(Note:) Please fill out and bring with you to your discussion with Rabbi Elkins. Each parent should fill out his or her own sheet. Be as brief or lengthy as you wish. It is important, however, to be honest, sincere, and personal - i.e., your own. There is no right answer. The purpose of the questionnaire is to facilitate meaningful discussion. Take as much thinking time as you need before writing, but don't let your inhibitions block out what you really want to write. Your meeting with the Rabbi will be more meaningful if you take the time and effort to fill it out. However, if you prefer not to, just write under any or all of the questions: "I prefer not to comment.")

1. I want my child to become Bar/Bat Mitzvah because _____

2. We belong to a synagogue because _____

_____

_____

_____

3. Jews are different from others in that _____

_____

_____

_____

4. The most important thing I want my child to learn in Religious School is _____

_____

_____

5. Religion is (important to me) (unimportant to me) because ____

_____

_____

6. I dream that _____

_____

_____

SELF-CONTRACT

(For further information about the Self-Contract, see **Values Clarification** by Sidney B. Simon, Leland W. Howe and Howard Kirschenbaum, Hart Publishing Company, pages 319-321.)

I, _____, in appreciation
           (print your name)
the true meaning of my Bar/Bat Mitzvah, will do the following things during the twelve months after my Bar/Bat Mitzvah:

1. _____

2. _____

3. _____

      Signed _____

      Reminder Date _____

      Witness _____

BEGINNING OF COMMITMENT/SUGGESTIONS

1. I will attend Shabbat morning services regularly.
2. I will continue in Hebrew High School at least to graduation (10th grade).
3. I will recite Kiddush and Motzi every Shabbat.
4. I will light the Sabbath candles and recite Motzi every Shabbat.
5. I will read at least six Jewish books each year.
6. I will attend a morning or evening minyan in the synagogue once a week.
7. I will actively participate in a synagogue-oriented youth group.
8. I will lead services when called upon to do so.
9. I will put on Tallit and Tephilin every morning.

10. I will take an active role in assisting my mother in preparing the weekly Shabbat meal.

11. I will learn the skill of reading the Torah and practice this skill in the synagogue service as called upon to do so.

12. I will keep kosher to the best of my ability outside of the house through eating no unkosher meat or seafood.

13. I will actively participate in Jewish social action programs.

14. I will carefully read the Sedrah of the week in the Torah - each week in English.

17
Values Clarification Strategies for Pesach

DEFINING VALUES CLARIFICATION

Values Clarification is a new field in education which has been making rapid strides in the past decade. It is extremely popular in school systems which are progressive and open to new ideas. Unfortunately, little or nothing has been done in the field of Values Clarification in Jewish education. Its potential is enormous, and the writer hopes to be publishing several items on applying the strategies of Values Clarification to the Jewish Home and Classroom, to tap this rich resource for Jewish education.

Two highly recommended books in this field are *Values and Teaching* by Louis E. Raths, Merrill Harmin and Sidney B. Simon (Charles E. Merrill, 1966, paperback) and *Values Clarification* by Sidney B. Simon and Howard Kirschenbaum (Hart Publishing Co., 1972, paperback). Both books are available from the National Humanistic Education Center, Upper Jay, N.J. 12987 ($4.25 each). Write also for their catalog of publications and workshops. My own participation in one of their week-long workshops last year has had

Published in *Alternatives in Religious Education,* Spring, 1976.

profound effects on my approaches to many areas of congregational work.

VALUES CLARIFICATION FOR PESACH

The following values clarification strategies can be used for adult or youth groups. They can be used before Pesach in the classroom, youth group or living room, or at the Seder Table.

Strategy One—*Visiting Our Seder*

Each person at the Seder Table (classroom, living room, study group) is asked to answer a question: How do you think _____ would react were he to visit our Pesach Seder this year? Leader assigns names to each participant. Examples: President Ford; Senator Jackson; Brezhnev, our gentile next door neighbor; Charlie Brown; Richard Nixon; Yitzchak Rabin; Henry Kissinger; your public school teacher; your law partner; the corner policeman; the Mayor of your city. For this discussion mention only the good things a visitor might see.

This strategy will produce good discussion, probably some good laughs, creative responses, maybe some deep and innovative thinking, and lots of new insights about ourselves, our Seder, and other people.

Strategy Two—*My Favorite Part of the Seder*

Leader to group: You have just concluded your Pesach Seder. Your school teacher (for adults, the neighborhood minister) has just come by to visit, not realizing it is a Jewish holiday. He is told that a Seder just took place. He asks you: Please tell me about one interesting part of the Seder. (Each person is now given a few minutes to write—or think if it is actually during the holiday—of his/her favorite part of the Seder, and why he/she likes it.)

Leader: OK, now that we've had a few minutes to compose our answers, let's go around and see what you came up with.

This strategy will help focus on the important ideas, experiences, colorful and meaningful rituals, and what significance they convey to each participant.

Strategy Three—*If You Were in Egypt*

Leader says to group: If you were in Egypt and were one of the average men/women in the street, an ordinary pyramid builder, how would you have reacted to Pharaoh's harsh treatment of the Israelites? (Goes around room, table, giving each person a chance to respond.)

Answers will range from writing a letter to the editor of the Egyptian Times-Union to blowing up Pharaoh's palace. Participants will be giving their views on political strategies to uproot injustice in society.

Follow-up discussion. What should American blacks do? Russian Jews? Syrian Jews? Women in any country? What might our family do to help oppressed minorities?

CONCLUDING NOTE

Use of these strategies will help the participant to analyze where he stands and what his values are. His/her choice of a Seder ritual or passage, analysis of the reaction of a fantasy visitor, or political strategy to fight oppression, will help that person know where he stands on vital issues. Each selection or analysis will disclose something about our preferences, our likes and dislikes, the things which are important to us - i.e., that which we *value*. Picking a passage in the Seder ritual, for example, will help a person clarify: a) what I prefer about the Seder ritual, b) what kinds of prayers move me, c) what types of rituals have contemporary meaning in my eyes, d) what level of personal involvement I find in this kind of religious activity.

18
A Jewish Consciousness Raising Workshop

The writer has undergone extensive training in individual and group therapy, humanistic psychology and education, encounter group and Gestalt workshops, human relations laboratories, and other experiences in human relations education, in a doctoral studies program as well as in one- and two-week workshops with some of the country's leading trainers in the Human Potential Movement, at such leading growth centers and consulting organizations as NTL, University Associates, the New England Center for Personal and Professional Development, with Sidney B. Simon, Merrill Harmin and Howard Kirschenbaum in values clarification, with Effectiveness Training Associates of Pasadena, California, and with Ridge Consultants for Maximizing Human Resources in Syracuse, New York, in communication skills for personal and professional effectiveness.

The design for the Jewish Consciousness Raising Workshop grows out of my training in all of the above areas over the past four years, as well as twenty years in Jewish education and twelve years in the rabbinate, as teacher, group leader, camp supervisor (Ramah), educator, lecturer, author and book critic, and facilitator of laboratory education.

It is my contention that much more of the new techniques in the behavioral sciences could be applied in the spheres of formal and informal adult and children's Jewish education, and Jewish community leadership development, and that we are overlooking a tremendous resource by not doing so. The whole field of psychology and education has been dramatically revolutionized over the past decade through new approaches now being used in progressive public and private education, creative industrial management and leadership training, and organizational development. It behooves the organized Jewish community to become more familiar with these advances, to take greater advantage of them in our own educational and community programming, and to engage qualified, Jewishly-committed experts as consultants to help train a corps of Jewish professional and lay leaders to utilize these new techniques, approaches and philosophies.

The design of the Jewish Consciousness Raising (J.C.R.) Workshop flows out of my own training and experience in this general field of human relations training. It is based upon the following six philosophical and behavioral science components.

Ideological Assumptions and Behavioral Science Components of Jewish Consciousness Raising [J.C.R.] Workshop
1. Existential Theology

From the works of Martin Buber, Franz Rosenzweig and Abraham Joshua Heschel comes the Jewish existential stress on personal responsibility for one's faith commitment, belief system, and intensive personal here-and-now relationship with God and fellow human beings. Man exists in community and must learn to treat others as "Thou" and not "It" - through existential relating rather than through objectification and manipulation. Through love and authentic human contact, persons can realize their best inner self. Through awareness of

God persons can bind their individuality with the ultimate purpose of human life and the universe.

2. Judaism as a Civilization

From the writings and teachings of Mordecai M. Kaplan and his disciples, Milton Steinberg, Ira Eisenstein, and others, comes the importance of *a priori* love of the Jewish people and a respect for an intense involvement in Jewish culture, mores, sancta, and the view of Judaism as more than religion—but rather as an evolving (growing, changing) religious civilization. Reconstructionism, as Kaplan called his philosophy, or Jewish religious humanism, as it is known among many, stresses the tremendous potential of man to fulfill himself, and to transcend his present self. It teaches a trust in God as the force for good in human beings and in the universe, and as the basis for overcoming despair, tragedy and evil. It rests upon modern, scientific, rational, democratic foundations which have come to be part of the American heritage. In the words of Rabbi Ira Eisenstein, "Religious humanism . . . implies that the spiritual life emerges from our full identification with the millenial process of Jewish existence."

3. Hasidic Judaism

Hasidic Judaism contributes significantly to the Jewish Consciousness Raising Workshop in several ways. Its stress on personal meaningfulness; spontaneity and joy in worship, learning and living; avoidance of rote and mechanical fulfillment of traditional *halacha;* overcoming the artificial dichotomies between the sacred and the profane; the ineffable awareness of God's presence in all things, and reachability of God through all pure deeds; deep love of all living creatures as unique and precious beings, as the primary path to love of God; stress on such values as fulfillment, ecstasy, service, intention, humility, redemption, devotion, and prayer; song, dance, feasting, fasting, pursuit of individual freedom, human dignity, as legitimate paths to spiritual growth.

4. Group Dynamics

The behavioral science of Group Dynamics has contributed considerably to our knowledge of large and small groups, in terms of their methods of functioning, stages of development, ways to strengthening a sense of community and group loyalty, and social interactional processes. Within the past two decades there has been a dramatic increase of interest in sensitivity groups, centers for personal and professional growth, workshop-laboratory learning, and other facets of what is now called the "Human Potential Movement." Through group process people learn to become aware of their own behavior, are able to overcome loneliness and isolation, and learn more constructive ways of being human. Some of the key elements in the process of personal growth emphasized in such groups are: enhancement of positive self-concept and the ability to assert oneself nonaggressively, two major components of the Jewish Consciousness Raising Workshop.

5. Humanistic Psychology

The new "Third Force" in modern psychology, founded by Abraham Maslow and others, Humanistic Psychology, views man as a total physical-mental-spiritual creature who lives in interrelationship with others. It posits a growth-orientation as man's basic instinct. It assumes that, given a nurturing environment, man will seek to expand his awareness and competence as a creative human being, and will be in an on-going process of learning, changing, adapting and growing. He is a creature of choice and will, who can overcome biological and sub-conscious obstacles to growth under proper conditions of self and outside nourishment.

6. Humanistic Education

Humanistic Education, an outgrowth of Humanistic Psychology, stresses learning and growth for the whole person, rather than just the mind. This includes education of the body, the emotions, the mind and the spirit. Most Jewish and general education today stresses education of the mind, almost to the total exclusion of the other three essential components of human existence. In traditional education today, the education and development of feelings, attitudes, values, philosophy of life, spiritual sensitivity and body awareness are all under-emphasized. Through effective humanistic education, the learner becomes more productive and creative in the essential areas of human life: thinking, feeling, choosing, communicating and acting. Building a strong self-concept is an essential component in humanistic education. Only a person who accepts himnself for who he/she is, and has a general sense of high self-esteem, can be a competent learner and can relate effectively to other human beings. The ability to assert oneself in a mature and appropriate way is a key building block in overall self-esteem. Mature acceptance of one's religio-cultural heritage is an essential element in developing a strong self-concept.

7.   Interactive Learning Process (I.L.P.)

A technique of humanistic education that is essential to open education, and to laboratory learning, is the Interactive Learning Process. Traditional education assumes a teacher and students, a leader and followers. The teacher/leader is presumed to be filled with information which is to be transmitted to the student/learner through talking and reading assignments. In the Interactive Learning Process, learning takes place not only from books and speeches, but from the total environment, group process, experiential events, structured learning models, such as case studies, role-plays, instrumentation, simulations, educational growth games, and intensive growth groups. Stress is placed on behavioral change.

The learner is responsible for creating his own learning goals and seeing that they get fulfilled to the best of his/her ability, is an active participant in the learning process - as learning comes from the group, from the structured experiences, as much as from the leader/teacher who in this model functions as facilitator of personal growth and social learning.

Goals of J.C.R. Workshop

1. To achieve intellectual understanding of some of the components that go into heightened awareness of Jewish identity, such as pride in one's heritage, the ability to assert one's ethnic and religious rights, and handling values collisions.
2. To establish closeness and warmth and meaningful person-to-person contact within the workshop learning community, as a microcosm of effective, organic Jewish community.
3. To experience the joy, ecstasy, enthusiasm and spontaneity of Jewish observance, worship and learning, through song, dance, meaningful prayer, relevant study, traditional observance of Shabbat and group interactive learning experiences.
4. To establish a norm of personal responsibility for one's Jewish beliefs, commitments and values, as modeled by personal responsibility for gaining significant learnings from this workshop, participation in planning and executing various facets of the weekend/Shabbat experience.
5. To learn new skills, techniques and programs for use in back-home spheres of Jewish family, educational, organizational, and community life.
6. To experience the pride, excitement, exhilaration and joy of making Judaism a living, vibrant aspect of one's life.
7. Examine our own personal values and priorities and analyze factors which impede stronger Jewish identity and commitment; as well as learning new ways to intensify personal Jewish values and commitments.

Design of the J.C.R. Workshop

The Jewish Consciousness Raising Workshop has three basic elements which will be carried out on (1) Friday night, (2) Shabbat afternoon, (3) Sunday morning. These are: Self-Acceptance (Enhancing Jewish self-esteem, ethnic pride and Jewish identity); Self-Assertion (Learning Assertion Skills for minority group members); Self-Awareness (Clarifying Jewish Values). (The eventual plan is to develop full weekend and/or week-long workshops for Jewish leaders in *each* of these three areas: self-acceptance, self-assertion and self-awareness).

In addition to the three main workshop sessions other important elements of the program are:

1. Planning and leading some of the worship experiences by group members (mimeographed explanation of prayers and creative prayers can be sent by myself or worked out with local rabbis).
2. Leading of prayers before and after meals, Shabbat candle lighting, Havdala services Saturday night by participants.
3. Planning and implementing Saturday night program on one of the three sub-themes to be done by the group under supervision of myself and/or local leadership.
4. Booklet of readings distributed in advance for members' preparation and deeper personal involvement.
5. All physical arrangements such as rooms, meeting halls, meals, registration, bringing Siddurim, Humashim, Torah scrolls, Havdala implements, name tags, etc. to be done by participants.
6. Posters, placards, designs, symbols, posted on walls of meeting rooms, prepared and posted by participants. Table signs with key phrases from the Sidrah of the week prepared and set up by participants.

Part I

Self-Esteem

Friday night will be spent on activities, structured experiences, mini-lectures and group discussion on the general theme of self-concept. Some of the themes and experiences included in this sphere are:

1. Definition of self-concept, self-acceptance, self-image, self-esteem
2. Effect of healthy self-concept on attitudes and behavior
3. Self-concept for individuals as well as for groups; ethnic identity, group price; assimilation, inter-marriage, life priorities, etc.

4. We're OK, You're OK - attitude to Americans, "goyim," Arabs, blacks.

5. Jewish anti-Semitism; Jewish self-hatred.

6. Validation training; appreciation of self and others.

7. Affirmation of self and Jewishness in small groups.

8. Zionism, State of Israel, Jewish nationalism, organic Jewish community, knowledge of Hebrew language and culture, meaningful Jewish observance, awareness of the Divine, as boosts for Jewish self-concept.

9. Use will be made of the writer's book, *Glad to Be Me: Building Self-Esteem in Yourself and Others* (Prentice-Hall, 1976).

Part II

Self-Assertion

Shabbat daytime will be spent on activities, structured experiences, mini-lectures and group discussions on the general theme of self-assertion, including the following themes and experiences:

1. Definition of Assertion and Assertivness Training
2. The assertion Continuum:

Submission	Assertion Protecting Space/ Impacting	Aggression
Assimilation/ Intermarriage	Anti-defamation; civil rights	Irgun
Self-Hatred	Zionism	J.D.L.
Passing	Religious, Cultural Commitment	PLO
	Aliyah	Fritz Fanon
	Hebrew Education	

3. Dealing with emotions, feelings, about one's Jewishness—dyadic and small group encounters (I-Thou meetings)
4. Protecting Space
   ADL, AJC, AJC Jewish Rights Council
   Community Relations Councils (CRC)
5. Impacting: Contributions to American society
   social responsibilty
   democracy, freedom, justice
   sanctity of individual
   culture and mores (art, music, custom, food, letters, drama)
   family strength
   Shabbat, holy days
   ethnic price
   organic community
6. Situational analysis - What would you do if. . . .
   Experiences that face us in our lives as Jewish in a Christian environment)
7. Personal styles of behavior - submissive, risk-taking, assertive, aggressive. What is mine?
8. Obstacles to being self-assertive
9. Risk-taking and non-verbal assertion exercises
10. Inviting others (individuals and groups) to modify their behavior. Assertion statements. Self-disclosure. "I" messages.
11. Assertiveness as life-style
12. The creative use of personal and group power

Part III

Self-Awareness

Sunday morning will be spent on activities, structured experiences, mini-lectures and group discussions on the general theme of self-awareness, with particular emphasis on becoming aware of one's Jewish values and life-style priorities.

The approach used is that of Sidney Simon, Merrill Harmin and Howard Kirschenbaum in their books, *Values and Teaching* (Merrill, 1966) and *Values Clarification—A Handbook of Strategies* (Hart, 1972).

Values Clarification strategies have been adapted by the writer in his handbook, *Clarifying Jewish Values*. Some of the strategies included are:

1. Twenty Jewish Activities You Love To Do
2. Jewish Values Grid
3. Percentage Questions
4. Sentence Completions
5. Jewish Values Whip
6. Proud Whip
7. Values Focus Game
8. Brainstorming
9. Jewish Coat-of-Arms
10. Letters to the Editor

This third area, Jewish self-awareness, is the logical development following Jewish self-esteem and Jewish self-assertion. When one is proud of one's religio-ethnic identity and is willing and able to assertively act on his values and commitments, then it becomes necessary to constantly clarify what one stands for as a Jew. This in turn reinforces one's self-esteem and channels the self-assertiveness in meaningful directions.

19
Jewish Values for Skilled Helpers

THE HUMANISTIC APPROACH

Jewish communal workers can be classified as skilled helpers, in Gerard Egan's terminology. This includes social workers, Federation executives, group facilitators, Jewish Center workers, family service counselors and case workers, rabbis, teachers, educators, and anyone else involved in human relationships. People who work with and help other people, if they are skilled, should have in their bag of skills a combination of knowledge in both behavioral science and Jewish law and lore.

During the past decade a new model in psychological theory has become increasingly popular: humanistic psychology and education. The humanistic approach is person-centered. It stresses the here-and-now, the whole person, and the subjective self, as opposed to psychoanalytic and behavioral schools that preceded them. In fact, since it followed those two schools of psychological thought (the work of Freud and Skinner), it is known as the "Third Force."

Humanistic psychology has become popular among skilled helpers since it is the first psychological model that is health- and growth-oriented, and since it stresses the joy of life, the fulfillment of human potential, self-actualization, and a value orientation towards life. It is popular among counselors and helpers who have a religious or religio-ethnic orientation since its approach closely parallels the approach of traditional religions. It avoids the anti-theological over-emphasis on man's sexuality and aggressive and violent tendencies, and on the materialistic and mechanistic schools of thought. Rather, it places stress on man's positive nature, his instincts for health, growth, meaning, fulfillment, self-transcendence, and valued living.

A convenient summary of the principles of humanistic psychology is found in Joseph Stein, *Effective Personality: A Humanistic Approach* (Brooks/Cole, 1972). Stein enumerates its essential principles as follows:

1) The person is worthy and inherently good.
2) The person's experience of his own self and of the world is his reality.
3) The person's psychological needs for love, belonging, creativity, and self-actualization are as innate as his physiological needs.
4) To understand human behavior, the person—not other animals—should be the chief object of study. And the person should be studied as a whole.
5) Although he is influenced by his past experience and the present environment, the person has the resources to make decisions and choices that do not repeat the past. Awareness, by means of which he anticipates outcomes, guides his choice.
6) Attitudes, values, and goals—distinctly human attributes—also guide the person's choice and reflect his philosophy of life.
7) Man is unique in the extent to which he feels kinship

with his own kind, in his belongingness, and in his concern for his fellowman.

8) In addition to being, the person has the potential for becoming.

JEWISH VALUES AND HUMANISTIC PSYCHOLOGY

The above description of the new third force in psychology, which is the basis for the health model in the helping professions, is remarkably similar to Jewish traditional cultural norms and values.

The writer has assembled a fairly long list of Jewish value words and concepts that correspond in a remarkably close way to the terminology (and their ideological referents) current in the literature of humanistic psychology. Skilled helpers in the various professions of Jewish communal service would do well to familiarize themselves with some of these Jewish value concepts in order to better transmit a total sense of Jewishness in their work.

There is a strong trend today to encourage greater reliance and utilization of Jewish value schemes in Jewish community work. It is becoming a recognized fact that the more assimilated, the less Jewish, individuals and families become, the closer they come to the higher levels of alcoholism, divorce, delinquency, and other social problems which are reflected in general society. It thus behooves Jewish communal workers to familiarize themselves more deeply with Jewish value concepts as they relate to the helping skills they use in their work, towards the goal of restoring Jewish values to the Jewish individual, family and community.

The list below of Hebrew value words, which are concepts frequently referred to in the helping professions, are freely translated to correspond to related terms in the humanistic approach to the applied behavioral sciences. It is my firm conviction that the freely translated phrases and terms do not distort the basic meaning of the Hebrew original.

HEBREW VALUES VOCABULARY
FOR JEWISH COMMUNAL WORKERS

1. *Mitzvah*—growth-motivated acts (as opposed to deficiency-motivated, in Maslow's terminology); an act producing Being Values; an act promoting self-actualization and social betterment.
2. *Simcha, oneg*—joy, fun, playfulness, pleasure, healthy child (in T.A. terms)
3. *Shabbat*—day for satisfying growth needs; a day for higher need (meta-need) satisfaction, as well as other personal and social needs: food, shelter, community, love, esteem.
4. *Teshuva*—Personal growth; flexibility; value prioritizing; self-actualization; fulfilling one's potential.
5. *Brit*—Covenant; valuing community; team-building; contract.
6. *Torah*—Law; knowledge; justice; growth of intellect; transpersonal awareness; Weltanschauung.
7. *Shalom*—Wholeness, holism, Gestalt; fullness.
8. *Nefesh*—Personhood; mind-body holism; absence of dichotomies.
9. *Beracha*—Awareness; awe; gratitude; transcendence.
10. *Chayt*—Sin; not fulfilling one's potential; fearing our own greatness; humanistic guilt (awareness of need for growth and improvement).
11. *Chesed*—Being-value; altruism; self-transcendence; love; mercy; compassion.
12. *Chag*—Holy day; peak experience; reaching highest potential.
13. *Kodesh, kedusha, kaddish*—holiness, sanctity; uniqueness; sacralization of the ordinary; awe; dignity of persons.
14. *Halacha*—Order; structure; organization; unity; purposefulness; meaning.
15. *Machloket le-shem shamayim* (Controversy for the sake of Heaven)—Healthy conflict; open system; openness; congruence; open communication.
16. *Talmid Chacham, Rav*—Teacher; example, role model; guru; therapist; wise man, sage; charismatic leader.

17. *Emet*—Truth; authenticity; honesty; purity.
18. *Bar/Bat Mitzvah*—Owning responsibility; taking charge of one's own life; responsible behavior; maturity; self-support.
19. *Ahava she-ayno tluya be-davar* (love which is not dependent on another factor)—unconditional positive regard; empathy.
20. *Ahavat Ha-Briyot*—Altruism; love of mankind; esteem for others; dignity of personhood.
21. *Hevay makdim b'shlom kol adam* (be first to greet your fellow)—Risk-taking; congruence; openness.
22. *Kavanah*—Intention; concentration; full awareness; being fully present; here-and-now; existential living; active listening.
23. *Le-Chaim*—Joy of living; positive, growthful view of life; respect for physical pleasure; physical/spiritual wholeness.
24. *Chaver, Chevra, Chavurah*—Fellowship; community; teamwork;team/community building; companionship; sharing; intimacy; friendship; opportunity for catharsis.
25. *Be-tzelem Elohim* ("I'm the image of God")—Dignity of human beings; holiness of life; instincts for growth and greatness; uniqueness of persons.

CONCLUSION

There are many more Hebrew words, phrases, expressions, concepts, and ideas which correspond very closely to the vocabulary of the human potential movement and humanistic psychology. The above list is merely a sample of some of them. They should be explored and studied for further coalescence of Jewish and human values, with a view toward helping skilled helpers in Jewish communal agencies reflect and teach their own cultural and religious heritage.

20
Community Building in the Classroom and Other Groups

GETTING ACQUAINTED

Form groups of three (triads). Try to pick two people you know least. Teacher facilitates group formation to avoid rejection feelings. Each person takes two or three minutes (start with shorter time periods) to tell others about him/herself.

Next, A and B tell C what they heard him/her say, and what they conclude about what was said or left unsaid. Instruct children to be helpful and supportive rather than critical or confrontative.

Each person can tell others something good he/she did this summer. This activity encourages ego-building and relationship-strengthening.

COCKTAIL MIX

Each student takes 8½ x 11" sheet of paper with question, "Who am I" written on top—large letters. In ten minutes write five key phrases which describe you. Legibility is important. Sheets are then pinned with safety pin on chest. Participants walk around, as at a cocktail party, without talking, reading each other's "Who am I?"

Students are to select one person they would like to talk with more, and they break into dyads (groups of two) for five minute conversation about the five phrases on the sheet. (Some will be pick*ers* and some pick*ees*—naturally not everyone can talk with first choice person.)

DEVELOPING THE "GROUP FEELING"

To develop a sense of group closeness and affection, this activity allows students to talk to one another in an informal non-threatening atmosphere about themselves as people.

Teacher explains that talking about our lives and experiences, of sorrow and joy, helps bring a sense of warmth and closeness. Students sit in a circle to facilitate effective conversation. Focus is on sharing experiences, not opinions. Thus, no argument, answers, or elaboration is necessary. One only needs to listen. Some conversation starters:

A funny thing that happened to me. . . .
Five years from now I. . . .
My pet. . . .
A time when I was sad. . . .
I miss. . . .
Someone I love is. . . .
Something about me I plan to change this year is. . . .
On Rosh Hashanah, my family. . . .

MY HOUSE

A map of your city is drawn on the blackboard or a real map posted on the wall. Students go to board (or map) and write their name approximately where they live (or pin a piece of paper with their name on their street on the map).

Students may then tell a few things about their block,

their neighborhood, their public school, or someone that lives next door.

Another advantage of this activity is finding out who lives near whom so that friendships can be formed outside the classroom; teacher and students can designate people to deliver homework assignments when students are absent or ill; carpooling can be arranged; and best of all, small intra-class support groups can be formed.

WHO AM I?

Post a sheet of newsprint on the walls for each participant/student. Each person takes crayon or magic marker and writes:

1. First name in English.
2. First name in Hebrew.
3. Parents' names in Hebrew and English.
4. Siblings' names in Hebrew and English (and ages).
5. Your favorite Hebrew letter.
6. Your favorite Hebrew word.
7. Your favorite Hebrew ritual (havdalah, candle-lighting, etc.).
8. Your favorite Jewish holiday.

A good way to handle this activity is for all students to write their information simultaneously, and then one at a time go up, stand next to his/her sheet of newsprint, read what is written, and have the group ask questions about any of the things written. Student standing at his sheet is interviewed like a "press conference."

Another way to do this is for one person to write his sheet at the beginning of each session, taking twenty sessions or so, until each student has had a turn being "interviewed."

DRAWING SHABBAT

Each student takes crayons and paper and draws his family at Friday night dinner table. When finished, students walk around the room holding up drawings and showing them to each other without speaking.

They are then asked to find three or four other people to talk to about what they drew. Each person takes a turn explaining his drawing. Each subgroup can select one person to share with the whole class some of the interesting things that came out of the subgroup discussion, in a summary way.

The above ideas were adapted from *Handbooks of Structured Experiences for Human Relations Training,* in 5 volumes, University Associates, Publishers, 7596 Eads Avenue, La Jolla, California.

PART III
Humanizing the Inner Life

21
Criteria for Healthy Religion

How mature, how healthy, how elevated is our religious belief and behavior? What ways are available to us to lift ourselves to a higher level of theology and religious action?

Critics of religion have charged, and often with great truth on their side, that religion has been a stultifying and inhibiting force in life. It sometimes dwarfed and perverted people instead of enlarging and beautifying their existence.

Such criticism reflects much truth because, in history, people have often behaved immaturely, and the level of their religious life naturally coincided with the rest of their personality. Abraham Maslow once said that only one person in a thousand really reaches a level of self-actualization. Why then should more than that proportion reach a high degree of religious maturity when society has remained so immature, so unfulfilled, so unhumanized?

Gordon Allport wrote in his book *The Individual and His Religion* (1950, p. 52):

A person of twenty, thirty, or even seventy years of age does not necessarily have an adult personality. In fact, chronological age is a comparatively poor measure of mental and emotional maturity, likewise of religious

171

maturity. In emerging from childhood, one gives up the egocentricism of his thought and feeling only under pressure, and, ordinarily, environmental pressure does not force a maturity of religious outlook upon the individual as inexorably as it does other forms of maturity. For the individual's religion is usually regarded by others as his own business and, so far as others care, can easily remain egocentric, magical and wish-fulfilling. Hence, in probably no region of personality do we find so many residues of childhood as in the religious attitudes of adults.

Agreeing with this analysis is Dr. Erich Fromm, whom I quoted yesterday in another connection, who predicts that "If we scratch the surface of modern man we discover any number of individualized primitive forms of religion. . . . One might just as well call them by their respective religious names: ancestor worship, totemism, fetishism, ritualism, the cult of cleanliness, and so on." (1950, p. 29)

If we consider religion to be that which occupies our "ultimate concern," as the noted theologian Paul Tillich did, then for many of us our religion is success, power, prestige, grades, love affairs, and a host of other modern idolatries.

If modern society abuses its religious heritage and places its ultimate concern in things of stone and concrete, how much more so did ancient and medieval persons whose fanatic religious beliefs led them to sanction, or even initiate, war, prejudice, witchcraft, sorcery, poverty, and injustice in the name of their Deity. Religious leaders have organized inquisitions, heresy trials, excommunication and torture chambers for the unbelievers of their day.

Let us examine, then, some criteria for a mature and healthy religious faith for a modern, scientifically-oriented rationally-grounded person of the last quarter of the twentieth century. And while we examine some of these criteria we can measure our own religious lives against them.

The first criterion I would establish for a mature, healthy religious faith is that it be related to today's needs, that it be fitting and appropriate for its adherent. If one accepts a tradition uncritically and carries it out in every detail only for the sake of perpetuating a tradition, without careful reflection on its meaning, purpose and relation to one's life, then that person's religion is low-level religion, and not mature, healthy religion. That is more the practice of magic than an act of faith, the repetition of habit rather than an existential commitment.

Dr. Clark Moustakas has written eloquently on the disastrous effects of habit on life, and his remarks can easily apply to the unreflected life of habitual religious practice and belief (1968, pages 15-16):

> To remain in touch with oneself as an individual requires an awareness of the conditions in society that threaten to chain man to a life of security and comfort, to a life of habit and routine, where feelings are modulated and disguised. Once a fixed pattern of living is established, the person only dimly perceives his own inner response to experience, his own real thoughts and feelings. He only vaguely notices that increasing regularity exacts a penalty of monotony and dullness and that organization and efficiency often lead to boredom. . . . As long as habit and routine dictate the pattern of living, new dimensions of the self will not emerge; new interests will not develop. The human scene becomes one of still life, where familiar images become commonplace and words and gestures repeat a well-known refrain. In such a state, it takes a sudden jolt to shock the person into an awareness that his existence is basically mechanical and dead.

To prevent mature religion from deteriorating to the level of childishness and idolatry, it is necessary to keep in mind the distinction between the needs of an active religious faith, and those of institutions which serve religious faith. When one serves only an institution and forgets the underlying purposes for which it stands, it is easy to lose sight of the true nature of mature faith.

The Talmud comments on the episode of Moses carrying the Ten Commandments to the people from Mt. Sinai. When the great Prophet saw the Israelites dancing around the golden calf, he smashed the tablets to the ground. The rabbis expressed shock at this outstanding leader treating the word of God with such disdain. They explained that when Moses saw the idolatry of the Israelites, the letters took flight and left the Tablets, soaring back to Heaven. Then the stone became so heavy that they dropped to the ground, for it was the letters that held them aloft. What they were saying is that when a religious institution loses its sacred purpose and denies the basic teachings of its faith, what is left is nothing but a cold, heavy structure, stone with no inner spirit of sanctity and spirituality, and that in time that structure will destroy itself by indifference to its own principles.

Maurice Friedman, the Jewish theologian who has translated and interpreted the works of Martin Buber for English-speaking audiences, has recently commented upon Buber's remark that "Religion is the great enemy of mankind." "By 'religion,'" explained Friedman, "Buber meant the tendency of every organized religion throughout history to promote and sanction a dualism that obscures the face of God and leaves our ordinary lives unhallowed and unhallowable." What Buber fought against was the "tendency to make of religion a separate upper story of spirituality with no binding force in our lives." (Moore, 1974, page XIII)

Another interpreter of Buber, Father Donald J. Moore, a Jesuit priest whose study of Buber was just published by the Jewish Publication Society, explains Buber's conception of healthy, dynamic, and relevant religion in these words (Moore, 1974, page 56):

> If man remains true to his attempt to seek constantly a response to the divine, he cannot take refuge in dogma, in any kind of once-for-all understanding of divine revelation. The dialogical view of history, which is the biblical view, seeks to preserve the mystery of the dialogical encounter between God and man from all tendencies toward rigid dogmatism. One cannot deny the existence of dogma in Judaism, but dogma remains always of secondary importance to that which is primary: the encounter between God and man. Dogma arises only after man turns aside from the lived moment, and the dogmatist too easily mistakes this detachment from the concrete situation as superior to the lived moment itself. Religious truths are dynamic; they can be understood only in the dynamic of their changing forms.

The first criterion, then, of healthy religion, is that it be free of entrenched habit, that it be close to the current needs of its adherent.

The second criterion for mature, healthy religion is that it be self-critical. Beware of a person who is totally certain that he has the truth, that his way is the best, that his faith is pure and unalloyed. Such a person, who does not occasionally doubt his beliefs, question his assumptions, re-open his belief system for critical examination, is resting his faith on a shaky foundation.

Mature faith is a "gamble on the unprovable based on (one's) integration of tradition, experience and reason. By itself, none of these tributaries to the stream of faith is adequate. Tradition and experience and reason all contribute to a vital faith." (Bolton, page 28)

Even in the realm of the hard sciences, such as physics,

there can hardly be any final certainty. Nobel prize-winning scientist Werner Heisenburg formulated the so-called "Uncertainty Principle" which makes it clear that one can never be absolutely certain about anything (Bolton, page 37): The principle of "Uncertainty" does not imply that religious belief can hide behind ambiguity and avoid the rigors of logical thinking. What it does mean is that after all the data is carefully examined, one can then take his leap of faith, based on reasonable, though unprovable, assumptions.

Gordon Allport elaborates on this theme: "It is characteristic of the mature mind that it can act wholeheartedly even without absolute certainty. It can be sure without being cocksure. We are not positive that we shall be alive tomorrow, but it is a good hypothesis to proceed on. . . . Faith is a risk, but everyone in some way or other is bround to take it." (Allport, 1960, page 72)

That is why, to me, Conservative Judaism speaks to American Jewry in more relevant terms than any other movement in American Jewish life. It is critical, flexible, developing, and yet based on a healthy regard for tradition and the past. During the past thirty years some major religious laws have been modified regarding the status of woman, Sabbath observance, laws of Kashrut, the marriage ceremony, the liturgy and other areas. We have followed the tradition in theological matters of granting enormously wide latitude and flexibility to individuals to locate themselves on the theological spectrum in a position most comfortable to themselves. New ideas of the meaning of God, new interpretations of divine revelation, new definitions of life in the hereafter and the Messianic Age, have all been expressed and accepted by large segments of American Jewry affiliated with Conservative synagogues.

The person who stops being critical, who ceases to doubt his religious stance, who leads an unexamined religious life, is existing on a low level of religious maturity.

The third criterion for healthy religion, for me, is that one's faith must have specific moral consequences. Someone once said that the function of religion is to comfort the afflicted, and afflict the comfortable. It is not enough to draw solace, strength, and stability from religious belief and practice, until one translates that personal growth into social awareness and moral responsibility (Clinebell, 1972, page 49).

Religious leaders in the Bible not only had a strong set of convictions, trust in God and man, but also felt deep responsibility for the amelioration of the lot of suffering humankind. The Biblical prophet had a sense of commitment to eradicate poverty, hunger, injustice, oppression and violence. From Abraham, who opened his home to the stranger, to Moses who taught a Torah of justice and compassion, through Elijah, Amos, Isaiah and Micah, all God's warriors on the stage of ancient Biblical history were fighters for standards of decency and fairness and carriers of love and values to their fellow human beings. They were standard bearers in the march toward human progress and societal wholeness.

Not always, however, have America's churches and synagogues carried out their moral duties as befits religious leadership. We Jews know of the silence of the churches in the 1930s and 1940s when Nazism raised its vicious head abroad and wiped out a third of our people. We know of their silence in the face of discrimination and persecution of our fellow Jews behind the Iron Curtain and in the face of attempted genocide in the Middle East.

But we, too, are not entirely blameless in this sphere. Neither are we totally clean when measured by the criterion of deep moral commitment. In fighting the scourge of the Vietnam War, in doing battle against racism, in helping to eliminate poverty in Appalachia and other scarred areas of our country, how far did our Jewish ideals drive us in joining the war against the eternal plagues of an unredeemed society? How healthy was our total religious gestalt in producing demonstrable moral behavior among members of the Jewish community?

What Martin Luther King, Jr. said about Christianity applies equally to us: "How often has the church had a high blood count of creeds and an anemia of deeds?"

The moral concommitant of religious belief of which I speak should "derive from a sacred anger, a divine discontent with injustice, bigotry, ignorance, poverty, intolerance, and war. It (should) be nurtured by a compassionate regard for every living thing, and (should) be sustained by the universal love not only for God, but for the dignity and the sanctity of man, created in the divine image" (Silverman, 1967, page 108).

The fourth, and last, requisite for mature religion is that its consequences in the daily life of its adherent should be seen in the zest, joy, and spiritual strength of that individual. It will be seen in the over-all quality and vitality of one's life. If one is bored, listless, directionless, meandering through life as a bear in the forest, his religion is not providing him what it should.

In Sidney Jourard's words, "A religious orientation is healthy if it enhances life and fosters growth of one's powers as a human being, including the power to love, to be productive and creative. Thus, no matter whether a person be Christian, Jew, Moslem, Hindu, or Buddhist, the criterion of whether his religion is healthy is provided not by the piety and scrupulosity of his ritual observances, but by its effect upon life. Is he a vital, loving, strong, growing person who does not diminish others? Or is his piety accompanied by prudery, inability to love others, and lack of joy in living" (Jourard, 1974, page 309).

The deeply religious person will spend his life searching for tentative answers to life's ultimate questions, never being fully satisfied that he has found them. This search will provide for him an opportunity to grow as a person, to reach out to fellow humans in an I-Thou relationship, and to share together in satisfaction, exultation, and celebration some of the partial answers which they discover together.

Such a person will not be totally demoralized by defeat or failure, will not be permanently crushed by death or tragedy, and will not succumb to cynicism or despair in the face of corruption and evil in government or in the private sector. He will have the faith and spiritual power to snap back from temporary setbacks to himself, his family, his community, or his country. He will see life steady and whole. He will be expressive with his emotions, giving of his essence, understanding of others who are less endowed than he, and not grossly envious of those greater or stronger than he. He will accept the inevitability of change, knowing that the more things change, the more they stay the same. He will be in touch with his own inner being, trust his own instincts, have a healthy respect for his own ability and total self. He will maintain an alive and spontaneous attitude toward people and experience, and will never permit the past to chain his hands. He will freely share of his means, time, and love, and yet be prepared to defend his own space and rights when necessary. He will freely admit when he is wrong and have the courage to stay the same when change is not called for.

In short, life for a person with a mature faith, will be an experience of searching, growing, sharing, loving, enjoying, and perpetual reaching for more and better, always knowing that he will never attain his highest goals nor totally realize his fondest dreams.

If religion can help a person find this creative attitude to daily living, it is healthy religion, and one that is worthy of being passionately cared for, intensely studied, and zealously practiced and experienced on the deepest possible level by a modern Jew.

22

Kavanah as Existential Living - Judaism and the "Here and Now"

I have been preoccupied during the past several years in my reading, thinking, writing and speaking about the question of "What makes a meaningful life?" Recently I rediscovered that an old Hebrew concept contains the seeds for unfolding one of the most germinal ideas in modern thought for a mature, purposeful, and energetic existence.

The ancient rabbinic concept of "Kavanah", I find, is very closely related to what modern existential theologians as well as humanistic psychologists refer to as living in the "here and now."

Thus, my message on this first morning of the New Hebrew Year, is to explore one of the keys to finding a more significant, more zestful, more satisfying way of life, religiously, emotionally, existentially. As in so many other instances, the ancient Hebrew sages anticipated the insights and discoveries of the most modern students of human behavior.

The word *Kavanah* has several levels of meaning. It is variously translated as "intention" and "motivation," on the one hand, and "devoutness" and "concentration" on the other. According to our revered teachers, prayer and mitzvot should be performed with sincerity, with motivation, with concentration, with the proper intention, and with devoutness. Some rabbis even went so far as to say that performing a mitzvah without kavanah is without total merit. Surely, they all agreed that the act of prayer must be accompanied by giving of oneself fully and totally to that activity with all-involving concentration.

The Shulkhan Arukh warns us, "Tov m'at be-kavanah me-harbeh blee kavanah," or "Better is a little with kavanah than a lot without it." The Eighteenth Century Hasidic work called *Tanya* states: "Tefillah b'lo kavanah ke-guf blee neshama," or "Prayer without kavanah is like a body without a soul."

Most insistent of all the rabbinic scholars on the presence of kavanah in prayer was Maimonides, who, despite his strong neo-Aristotelian rationality, shows himself to be a mystic at heart when it comes to communication with the Divine Presence, the Shekhinah. In his Code of Law, he writes (Tefillah 4:16): "Kavanah means that the worshiper must clear his mind of all private thoughts and regard himself as standing before the Shekhinah. If his thoughts are wandering or occupied with other things, he should not pray . . . . Prayer should be accomplished quietly and with feeling, not like one who is trying to unload a burden and departs as soon as he gets rid of it."

In his other *magnum opus,* the *Guide for the Perplexed,* which is Maimonides' major philosophical treatise, he deals with the proper approach to the recitation of the two most significant prayers in the Hebrew liturgy, the Shma and the Amidah (3:51):

"The first thing you do is this: Turn your thoughts away from everything while you read Shema or during the Tefillah . . . After some time, when you have mastered this, accustom yourself to have your mind free from all other thoughts when you read any portion of the other books of the prophets, or when you say any blessing . . . When you are engaged in the performance of religious duties, *have your mind exclusively directed to what you are doing.*"

In that paragraph, Maimonides hints to us that the behavior which is appropriate for prayer and study is also most fitting for other religious acts and duties—namely, having one's mind free from all other things and having it directed exclusively to what one is doing at this very moment.

More and more in recent years, students of human life and human development have been finding this key of full concentration, of being fully present where you are, as the basis of meaningful living.

Some twenty years ago, Erich Fromm wrote his classic little volume for the World Perspectives Series called *The Art of Loving* (1956). In it, he tells his readers that loving another human being is an art and a skill which must be carefully cultivated, like any other delicate art and skill. To master any art, he explains, requires a great measure of concentration. But in our culture, we are taught the opposite of concentration. "You do many things at once," explains Fromm. "You read, listen to the radio, talk, smoke, eat, drink. You are the consumer with the open mouth, eager and ready to swallow everything—pictures, liquor, knowledge. This lack of concentration is clearly shown in our difficulty in being alone with ourselves. To sit still, without talking, smoking, reading, drinking, is impossible for most people. They become nervous and fidgety and must do something with their mouth or hands. . . ."(Fromm, 1956, pages 108-9). We have heard countless times of people who try to quit smoking only to find that they increase their eating activity.

For healthy, mature and meaningful life, Fromm advises this prescription: ". . . one must learn to be concentrated in everything one does, in listening to music, in reading a book, in talking to a person, in seeing a view. The activity at this very moment must be the only thing that matters, to which one is fully given. If one is concentrated, it matters little *what* one is doing; the important, as well as the unimportant things assume a new dimension of reality, because they have one's full attention." (Fromm, 1956, page 113).

Fromm's teaching coincides with some of the most important teachings of Hasidic Judaism, which stress full enjoyment and immersion in life "here and now" rather than in some future far-off dream world. Martin Buber in his classic collection, Tales of the Hasidim, (1947, I, page 3), explains: "The hasidic movement did not weaken the hopes in a Messiah, but it kindled . . . its . . . followers to joy in the world as it is, in life as it is, in every hour of life in this world, as that hour is. Without dulling the prick of conscience . . . , hasidism shows men the way to God who dwells with them. . . ." According to Buber, Hasidism could be summed up in a single sentence: "God can be beheld in each thing and reached through each pure deed." It was the excitement of each moment, the newness of each experience, that made life exciting, challenging and daring, according to the Hasidic view of Judaism.

One of the disciples of Rabbi Moshe of Kobryn (died 1858) was asked, "What was most important to your teacher?" The disciple answered, "Whatever he happened to be doing at the moment." (Buber, 1948, II, page 173) In Buber's study of the Hasidic tradition (1958, pages 172-3), he relates: "It is said of a certain Talmudic master that the paths of heaven were as bright to him as the streets of his native town. Hasidism inverts the order stating that, it is a greater thing if the streets of a man's native town are as bright to him as the paths of heaven. For it is here, where we stand, that we should try to make shine the light of the hidden divine life.

"If we had power over the ends of the earth, it would not give us that fulfillment of existence which a quiet devoted relationship to nearby life can give us. If we knew the secrets of the upper worlds, they would not allow us so much actual participation in true existence as we can achieve by performing, with holy intent, a task belonging to our daily duties. Our treasure is hidden beneath the heart of our own home."

Scholars have pointed out that real genius consists of utilizing one's talents fully and completely by concentrating on acts of creativity. All the talents in the world will not bring achievement without the added significant cutting edge of total concentration. In Schiller's words, "Genius is concentration" (Perls, 1969, page 92).

Existentialist philosopher Martin Buber recounts the story of how he first came to discover his popular new philosophy of human relationships which he calls "I-Thou", a relationship of full devotion and concentration. He had counseled a young man who left the scholar's study unsatisfied and a short time later took his own life. That experience was seminal in Buber's discovery of the importance of a full human-to-human encounter, an I-Thou meeting of full beings. Buber realized that he had not been fully listening to the young student, had not given him his undivided attention, and had therefore been unable to hear him fully, not to speak of answering his gnawing anxieties.

Fritz Perls, modern founder of Gestalt Therapy, found his remarkable success with his clients in what he came to call "Concentration Therapy" (1969, pages 185 ff.). He discovered that when he was able to get his clients to focus their total awareness in the present moment, and cease unproductive historical ruminations and stop constantly blaming themselves over past mistakes, then a certain magic would take place in their psychic health. By giving full concentration to the act of the present moment, through attention to internal silence, body concentration, and other related techniques, he was able to help his clients regain their sense of aliveness and energy and hopefulness (Shepard, page 50).

It seems that the penetrating insights of the ancient and medieval Jewish sages were far in advance of their time when they stressed the importance of not trying to do more than one thing at one time. It is such a simple and obvious idea, yet one which, if carried out fully, could literally transform a person's total life.

All of us can tell of stories of people in the helping professions who gave less than their all to their clients, students, or patients, and seemed to be preoccupied with other things instead of giving full attention to the problems at hand.

All of us can think of times when members of our family were too busy daydreaming about the future, or romanticizing about the past, instead of giving themselves to the person with whom they were speaking or relating.

All of use can think of occasions when, instead of being helpful to those we love, to friends, or to charges, we were wrapped up rehearsing past events, or mentally preparing for future tasks, instead of living in the "here and now."

An important distinction must be made between being concerned with the past and the future and being consumed by them. It is good to take direction from our past history and personal lives. It is good to make plans for days and years ahead, to work toward a far-off goal. The mistake we make is living *in* the past, or *in* the future, instead of merely living *for* them. What we must learn to do is to live *in the present* and the present *only.*

Dr. Joseph Stein makes a similar point when he suggests that to find a more productive way of life people who have become accustomed to live in the past or in the future must redirect their life patterns. Such a person "needs to undertake sex for the sake of sex, not to prove he is a good lover; to work largely for the sake of work, not just to support his family; to have friends for the sake of friendship, not to make connections to use in his business; to read to enjoy the excitement of ideas, not to be able to participate in conversations at social gatherings; to own a car as a means of conveyance, not to impress others with something he can scarcely afford. He deprives his life of zest and spontaneity when he fails to live existentially" (1972, page 90).

In *The Man of La Mancha,* Don Quixote advises:

> Take a deep breath of life
> and consider how it should be lived . . .
> Call nothing your own
> except your soul.
> Love not what you are,
> but only what you may become.
> Look always forward:
> In last year's nest, there are no birds
> this year.

Maimonides realized some seven centuries ago that one who is searching in last year's nest will not be able to contact His maker, or perform a meaningful good deed for his neighbor.

In the same way, Fritz Perls tells of the young man who had an engagement for dinner one evening at 9:00 with a lovely lady friend. He had an examination in college the next morning. He had planned to study from 7:00 to 9:00, and then go out to dinner from 9:00 to midnight. But between 7:00 and 9:00 all he could think about was his dinner date at 9:00, and thus did not succeed in studying properly for the exam. Then, when sitting at dinner with his young lady friend, he berated himself the entire time about the coming examination for which he had not prepared himself. In the earlier part of the evening, he lived in the future, instead of the present. Then, in the latter part of the evening, he lived in the past, with recriminations about his failure to study properly, and ruined his entire evening. Had he lived in the here and now, he might have studied from 7:00 to 9:00, and having finished that, enjoyed his date from nine to midnight.

Dr. Jut Meininger speaks of the concept of "Time Competency" in his recent book, *Success Through Transactional Analysis* (1963, page 101). "The person," he writes, "who is time competent lives in the present, using information from his past and expectations of the future to enhance his perception of the present, not to limit it. The past and the future extend his perspective; they don't interfere with it. They help him plan, to assess probabilities, and to alter his present actions and his commitments to the future in terms of how he sees those probabilities. They broaden his understanding of the relationship between events—his sense of continuity between what has been, what is, and what is yet to be. Above all, the past and the future help the time competent person rather than hinder him."

How many people do we know who live in either the past or the future, wasting their precious days here on earth without savoring the sacredness of the present hour.

Some who live in the past beat their breast over foolish mistakes, wrong decisions, poor judgments, wasted years, and unnoticed opportunities. When we live in the present, we are aware of past errors, admit them and learn from them, but don't constantly wallow in them.

When we live in the future, we hope for a better day or save for a dream vacation or fantasy home without ever stopping on the way to taste the joys and excitement of the journey to reach them. "Some day," we say to ourselves, "I'll begin to enjoy life." We work hard and save up time and money and ideas, and dream that life will some day suddenly and magically rain happiness upon us. When the truth is that the happy person must learn how to live meaningfully and joyfully as he plans and saves and hopes for even more happiness later on in life (Stein, 1972, page 37).

Dr. Jerry Greenwald gives good advice when he writes in his popular study, *Be the Person You Were Meant to Be* (1973, page 64): "Being obsessed with a wasted past does nothing but waste the present. Regrets are an exercise in futility which can go on forever. Living in the moment means experiencing to the fullest what is nourishing in the present. ("Today is the first day of the rest of my life.") The essence of living in the now is a continued awareness of our experiencing self. There is nothing impulsive or irresponsible in this attitude. Rather, it emphasizes the reality of living: effective emotional nourishment is possible only in the present."

In a sermon on Yom Kippur, the Hasidic Rabbi of Ger warned against self-torture: "He who has done ill and talks about it and thinks about it all the time does not cast the base thing he did out of his thoughts. . . .He will certainly not be able to turn, for his spirit will grow coarse and his heart stubborn, and in addition to this he may be overcome by gloom. What would you? Rake the muck this way, rake the muck that way—it will always be muck. In the time I am brooding over it I could be stringing pearls for the delight of Heaven. That is why it is written: 'Depart from evil and do good'—turn wholly away from evil, do not dwell upon it, and do good. You have done wrong? Then counteract it by doing right" (Buber, 1958, pages 164-5).

A similar story is told by the modern mystical philosopher now known as Ram Dass, nee Richard Alpert (Ram Dass, 1974, pages 61-64). A promising young Jewish Harvard professor became enticed with Indian religion and found that everything he had done in his life to that time was in the wrong direction. He discovered in India what he might have discovered in the Talmud or from Maimonides and Hasidism, but his autobiography nevertheless provides a fascinating example of the importance of existential living, of living in the "here and now."

He tells of a visit to his wealthy father, just after his mother's death. His father was a conservative Boston Republican who had been President of the New Haven Railroad and a major contributor to Brandeis University and Albert Einstein Medical School. On the way home from the airport, his father speaks of his gloom and doom and how life is now totally without purpose for him. Arriving home, they decide to make raspberry jam, which was a hobby of his father's. While they sterilize the bottles and mash the raspberries, the father persists in his gloomy mood, speaking of how everyone has forgotten and neglected him.

Ram Dass ignores his father's talk of gloom and talks only of the raspberries. "Should the bubbles all rise to the top?" he asks. Soon his father, receiving no reinforcement for his dark cloud that he is creating and holding all by himself, gives it up, and turns his attention to the raspberries. "Well, get all the bubbles up," he warns his son. Very quickly the conversation turns to the here and now, the father relaxes and laughs, and the two of them find tremendous fun in making raspberry jam.

Ram Dass then completes the tale: "To short cut the whole story, let me explain that eight months later, I gave the bride away at his marriage . . . He married a . . . beautiful, wonderful woman. . . .As he went into the temple, he said to me, 'This is all your doing, you know,' because what I did was hold his hand all the time because all of his questions would be about the future or the past, like 'Is this wrong in terms of the memory of Mother? Is this going to be a terrible thing later?' All I was saying was, 'How does it feel today? Did you have a good time at dinner last night? What are we doing today?" And he said, 'Oh, it's wonderful. She's a wonderful person . . . .' As soon as his mind stopped creating all that stuff about then and there, and he lived here and now, . . . he was having a ball. He was writing love songs and they went on a honeymoon in Scotland and Ireland."

Of course, the father had beautiful and wonderful memories of his first wife. But wallowing in gloom would surely not have served either those memories or himself very well. It took a "here and now" philosopher to recognize that, and to help his father live *for* the past and *for* the future, but still very much *in* the present.

It is obvious, then, that Maimonides' extension of the old rabbinic principle of Kavanah has implications for how we relate to others, how we treat ourselves, how we see our lives, and how we make our decisions. Let's stop rehearsing the good and the bad of our past to the point of making our lives too historical instead of vibrant and alive. Let's not only dream about what can be in some glorious far off year, but make it happen beginning this very hour.

In Saul Ansky's version of *The Dybbuk* he talks about the sacred nature of Yom Kippur, the holiest day of the year, when the holiest man of his people, the High Priest, steps into the Holy of Holies, the holiest place in the holiest city in the holiest land. "Once during the year, at a certain hour, these . . . supreme sanctities of the world were joined with one another . . . .

"Every spot where a man raises his eyes to heaven is a holy of holies. Every man, having been created by God in His own image and likeness, is a high priest. Every day of a man's life is a Day of Atonement, and every word that a man speaks with sincerity is the Name of the Lord" (quoted in *The Jewish Catalog,* 1974, page 5).

The Jewish way of achieving existential living, of living dynamically in the here and now, is to sanctify life in such a way that each of us every hour of every day is a high priest in the holy of holies on the Day of Atonement!!

Listen to the words of Richard L. Evans (quoted in Mark Link, 1972, page 11):

"There are fathers waiting until other obligations are less demanding to become acquainted with their sons. There are mothers who . . . sincerely intend to be more attentive to their daughters. There are husbands and wives who are going to be more understanding. But time does not draw people closer!! When in the world are we going to begin to live as if we understood that this is life? This is our time, our day . . . and it is passing. What are we waiting for?"

The ancient sage Hillel was very much tradition oriented, very much history oriented, and yet in the popular ancient collection of rabbinic sayings called Pirke Avot, his most significant and well-known maxim ends with four simple Hebrew words: Ve-im lo achshav, aymatay? If not now, when?

23

The Jonah Syndrome: Fulfilling Human Potential

The Book of Jonah, which we study each year on Yom Kippur, is pregnant with rich meaning to the discerning reader. It is a study of a human being who went astray and makes a good object lesson for the Day of Atonement. Jonah sinned and repented and thus became the model for all of us. He is the epitome of the fallible human being, who, nevertheless, learns from his errors and from them emerges into a better person.

What exactly was Jonah's sin? The biblical book explains that he did not fulfill God's charge to go and speak to the people of Nineveh, that great Assyrian capital, and warn them to repent. He failed to carry out God's mission.

The late Dr. Abraham Maslow, of Brandeis University, whom I consider one of the most revolutionary minds of the twentieth centry, recorded his own interpretation of Jonah's sin (Maslow, 1967, pages 162f). In a piece called "The Jonah Syndrome", Maslow explained that what Jonah did is what we all do—namely, we evade our highest destiny, we fear our own greatness, we run away from our own best talents.

Jonah was selected by God, just as dozens of prophets before him were singled out, because of his unique ability, his charismatic leadership qualities, his exemplary conduct in human affairs. He was singularly qualified to undertake a mission of education and indoctrination to the teeming metropolis of Nineveh and import to them of God's teachings of justice, equality, compassion, brotherhood, and human understanding.

And yet he paralyzed himself by fear, awe, and weakness. He felt himself unequal to God's task. He considered his shortcomings and inadequacies, and decided they were too great, that he was unworthy of this sacred mission.

Maslow explains that this pattern is a very human and widespread one, but one which prevents most of us from growing into the bigger and more highly evolved human beings we have the potential of becoming. In his words: "We fear our highest possibilities. . . .We are generally afraid to become that which we can glimpse in our most perfect moments. . . .We enjoy and even thrill to the godlike possibilities we see in ourselves in such peak moments. And yet we simultaneously shiver with weakness, awe, and fear before these very same possibilities."

He tells of saying to his students at the university, "Which of you in this class hopes to write the great American novel, or to be a Senator, or Governor, or President? . . . Or a great composer? Who aspires to be a saint, like Schweitzer, perhaps? . . . Generally," he explains, "everybody starts giggling, blushing, and squirming until I ask, 'If not you, then who else?'" He then recalls a picture he once saw in a psychology textbook, divided into two parts. "The lower half was a picture of a line of babies, pink, sweet, delightful, innocent, and lovable. Above that was a picture of a lot of passengers in a subway train, glum, gray, sullen, and sour. The caption underneath was very simply, 'What happened?' This is what I'm talking about."

One of the first people to recognize the fact that human beings were only living up to a fraction of their potential was Harvard professor William James, some three-quarters of a century ago. He made this observation: "I have no doubt whatever, that most people live whether physically, intellectually, or morally, in a very restricted circle of their potential being. . . .The so-called 'normal man' of commerce, so to speak . . . is a mere extract from the potentially realizable individual he represents, and we all have reservoirs of life to draw upon which we do not dream." (Goble, 1971, page 155).

I recall reading once that the sculptor who carved out of Mt. Rushmore the faces of four of our country's leading presidents was asked how he could accomplish such an enormous feat. He replied: "The figures were right there in the mountain. All I had to do was uncover the rock surrounding them." That, in a way, summarizes my message this evening. We all have within us marvellously etched features of brilliance and spiritual greatness. All we need do is get through the covers, to bore through the hard surface of fear and awe and trepidation and let it be seen before the world.

Jewish tradition has for millenia presented an image of man that was far higher than any other known conception among the religions, philosophies, and psychologies of the people of the world. Man was made but little lower than the angels (Psalm 8) in the image of God himself (Genesis 1:27).

The implications of this view of man are enormous! They have been read and taught for centuries, and yet only today are we beginning to fully realize the far-reaching consequences of seeing man as made in the image of God.

Dr. W. Ross Adey, of the Brain Research Institute at UCLA's Space Biology Laboratory, recently stated that "The ultimate creative capacity of the brain may be, for all practical purposes, infinite."

In a Russian publication dated November, 1964, Prof. Vasili Davydov of the Moscow Institute of Psychology reports that "As soon as modern science gave us some understanding of the structure and work the human brain we were struck by its enormous reserve capacity. Man, under average conditions of work and life uses only a small part of his thinking equipment. . . .If we were able to force our brain to work at only half its capacity we could, without any difficulty whatever, learn forty languages, memorize the large Soviet Encyclopedia from cover to cover, and complete the required courses of dozens of colleges." (Goble, 1971, page 159)

Martin Buber explained what this elevated conception of man means to him:

> Every person born into this world represents some-new, something that never existed before, something original and unique. "It is the duty of every person . . . to know and consider that he is unique in the world in his particular character and that there has never been anyone like him in the world, for if there had been someone like him, there would have been no need for him to be in the world. Every single man is a new thing in the world, and is called upon to fulfill his particularity in this world. . . ." Every man's foremost task is the actualization of his unique, unprecedented and never recurring potentialities, and not the repetition of something that another, and be it even the greatest, has already achieved (Buber, 1958, pages 139-140).

A rabbinic comment on the opening verse of the Bible, "In the beginning God made the heavens and the earth," explains that this means to say that God made the world in the beginning. In other words, He created it only in the beginning stages of development. It is man's task to perfect the world, and along with it to perfect himself and his own God-given talents and abilities.

Jonah's mistake, his sin, if you will, was that he conceived of himself as less than the image which Jewish tradition portrayed for him. He underestimated his own talents and capabilities. He ran away from his mission, his fate, his destiny.

The Hebrew word "Chet", which we repeat so many times on Yom Kippur in the confessional, does not really mean "sin" as we usually translate it. It means failure to reach the target, failure to hit the mark, failure to fulfill one's highest capacities. That was the sin of Jonah and that is our most grievous sin in life, our failure to realize our best selves.

One of the things that keeps us back from reaching our highest possible heights of self-realization is our dwarfed image of ourselves. Like Jonah, we emphasize our short-comings, our failures, our inadequacies, and overlook our strengths and our abilities. We lower our sights, and run away from our God-given tasks in life. We conceive of ourselves as inferior or incapable, and flee from our Nineveh to sail on a ship in fear and trepidation of our own mission. But if we are lucky, as Jonah was, we ultimately realize that we cannot flee from ourselves.

Sidney Jourard warns about creating too low a self-image of ourselves:

> Be careful what you believe to be true, because so long as you believe it, then for you it is true. . . .If you believe you cannot learn a musical instrument because you lack talent, get a musical instrument and learn it. If you believe you cannot do without food . . . (then) fast. Challenge your own beliefs, especially about yourself and others, because what you believe to be true . . . functions more as persuasion than as description
> (Jourard, 1974, pages 69-70).

A man who had committed a crime once appeared before Alexander the Great for judgment. The great king sentenced him to death. "I appeal," argued the defendant. "Appeal? To whom? I am the ultimate authority here!" "Your majesty," pleaded the condemned man, "I appeal from Alexander the Small to Alexander the Great!" On Yom Kippur, God calls on us to rise from being the small persons within us to the great and limitless potentialities within us.

Legend tells that there was once a frog, who was really a prince, who looked and felt like a frog. A spell had been cast upon him by a wicked witch, and only the kiss of a beautiful maiden could save him. But who wanted to kiss a frog? So there sat the unkissed prince who looked and felt like a frog. The fable ends, of course, in a pleasant way, when a lovely maiden appears and gives this frog a big smack, and crash, boom, zap, he becomes a dashing prince, and they lived happily ever after (Coleman, 1974, page 1).

Which leads me to the next point, that our conception of others affects the way they fulfill their potential. A friendly smile, a warm embrace, a kind compliment, can act as the kiss of life through which we turn a frog into a prince.

A Hasidic rabbi interpreted the word in the ancient priestly blessing, Ve-yishmerekha, as coming from the root "shemarim" or "yeast," and thus explaining the benediction to mean "May God create yeast in your soul, causing you to ferment, and mature, to rise, elevate, to your highest possibilities, to reach your highest self (Lamm, 1970, pages 10-11).

We can bless our loved ones in this way by adding the yeast, the leavening in their soul, which helps them rise to their highest self.

One of the impediments that Dr. Maslow suggests which prevents us from reaching higher than we normally do is our fear of being seen as arrogant. Perhaps Jonah thought to himself: "Who, me, a prophet? Who, me, accept a divine mission to represent Torah to the great thriving city of Nineveh? What arrogance that would be!"

Maslow says that we voluntarily cripple ourselves in a kind of mock humility, as a defense against sinful pride. But, he argues, there is a certain kind of self-pride that is not only justified, but crucial if we would reach our fullest potential. He writes: "To invent or create you must have the 'arrogance of creativeness'. . . .But. . . .if you have *only* the arrogance without the humility, then you are in fact paranoid. You *must* be aware not only of the godlike possibilities within, but also of the human limitations. You must be able simultaneously to laugh at yourself and at all human pretensions (Maslow, 1967, page 166).

I am reminded of the Hasidic admonition that a person must have two pockets in his coat, and in each carry a slip of paper containing an ancient Hebrew quotation. In one pocket the slip reads "For my sake the world was created" (Mishna Sanhedrin 4:5). In the other pocket it says: "I am but dust and ashes." (Genesis 3:19).

Another fear which prevents us from realizing our best selves is that we will have reached the climax of life too soon, we will have peaked out, done too much, reached too far beyond our time. We need something to hold out which is still not done, so we cripple ourselves, and hold back, and don't give our all.

But the truth is that we can stretch ourselves anew each time we reach a new and higher stage of accomplishment and being. The ultimate capabilities which we can reach are so far beyond us that instead of holding back, we ought to be stretching as high as we can, and then, reaching that new plateau, remain only until an even higher goal begins to beckon to us.

In George Bernard Shaw's words, "To have succeeded is to have finished one's business on earth, like the male spider, who is killed by the female the moment has has succeeded in his courtship. I like a state of continual *becoming*, with a goal in front and not behind."

We need never worry that if we reach too far, our business on earth will be finished. There is more in us than that. There is always another goal farther out, in the farthest reaches of human nature, which we can aspire to when we achieve the stage we thought would be the highest.

Let me describe two instances of people who acted in their lives differently than Jonah did when the Lord called them to a new misson. Instead of fleeing from themselves, instead of evading their destiny, instead of fearing their own greatness, instead of running from their own best talents, they decided to hear the inner call and act upon it.

First, a Polish-born naval officer named Jozef Teodor Konrad Korzeniowski, who was a veteran of eleven years in the British merchant marine. For a short period he was without a vessel and living in London. One morning without forethought, Korzeniowski sat down and began to write a story about a man he had met while sailing as a second mate on a steamship gathering rubber in Borneo. Korzeniowski later recalled, "Till I began to write that novel I had written nothing but letters, and not very many of these. I never made a note of a fact, of an impression, or of an anecdote in my life." All he had done was work hard to become an expert mariner, earning his captain's license and devoting himself to the sea.

Jozef Korzeniowski changed his name to Joseph Conrad and, at age 37, this seemingly contented mariner left the sea forever and became a writer of such classic novels as *Lord Jim, Youth,* and *Typhoon.* Writing not in his native tongue,

Polish, but in his acquired language, English (Good, 1974, page 147).

Another dramatic example of one who heard his inner call and instead of fleeing from his own greatness, sailed towards it and achieved it, is a young man who at age twenty-three was a stockbroker in Paris for the staid old financial house of Bertin and Company. He showed great ability in his work, had a good income, was married to a very respectable middle-class Parisian woman, and eventually raised five children.

Somehow, though, it wasn't enough. His mission was more than what he was doing. So he began to paint, at first only on weekends. His friends humored him for a while, but when he began to associate with the avante-garde Impressionists, who struck the "nice" people of the day as uncouth, they began to panic. At age 35, Paul Gauguin left all his comforts behind him and went to Tahiti to live and paint, and become one of the world's most acclaimed artists (Good, 1974, page 148).

Of course, for most of us, it does not necessarily mean changing careers or leaving home. Our own awakening sometimes comes after a serious illness, or after a long trip, or during a period of long solitude, or perhaps just during the day-to-day routine of living, when it suddenly dawns upon us that life has more in store for us than what we have contented ourselves with until now. It is time to stop fleeing from our destiny, our talents, our selves, and accept the divine call to become a greater, more fully human person.

Sometimes, it may be reading a special book, or seeing an exciting show, or meeting an unusual person; sometimes it could be experiencing an unusually deep adventure in prayer, or study; it could be the opportunity to deprive oneself of food for a full day and think only about our life and its purpose and destiny. Whatever the trigger, it is often necessary to shake ourselves out of our lethargy and break through the crust of habit and fear and dare to be our real selves.

Dr. Maxwell Maltz, a plastic surgeon, has written in his many books on psychocybernetics about the limitless changes that take place in people, who, through plastic surgery, suddenly see themselves differently. He realized after years of such surgery that it is not necessary to physically change our self-image, but that one can change one's self-appraisal by overcoming the fear of being what we can be. He writes:

> Did it ever occur to you that there is real greatness in you? Did it ever occur to you that this greatness awaits recognition—from you? Did it ever occur to you that you are your most important human being and that the famous people you read about in your newspaper are of no consequence compared to your importance to yourself? And, did it ever occur to you that in your uniqueness as a human being you have an uncommon potential, which you owe it to yourself to nurture, accepting yourself for what you are, refusing to model yourself on other people? (Maltz, 1973)

Thomas Edison was once watching the ocean, and as the waves rolled in, he cried and said: "So much energy going to waste. If only we could harness that power." We can say the same about ourselves. So much energy going to waste. If only we could harness our own spiritual power.

The sainted Rabbi Zussya was once asked, Zussya, when you reach the gates of heaven, are you not afraid that you will be asked, "Zussya, why weren't you like Moses, why weren't you like Akiba?"

"No," replied the sage, "I am afraid only that I will be asked, Zussya, why weren't you like Zussya? Why did you not achieve the best that Zussya could have been?"

That indeed is the meaning of our atonement on this holiest day of the year. Our greatest sin has been to ourselves. Our most serious failure is not having become what we might have become, and for running away like Jonah from what we promised ourselves last Yom Kippur.

On another Yom Kippur, some fifty years ago, the great philosopher Franz Rosenzweig visited a little schul in Germany as a last-minute gesture to affirm his decision to convert to Christianity. That experience stirred him so that he decided instead to study Judaism intensely and became one of the leading Jewish thinkers of this century. Just after that experience, he wrote a letter to a friend, in which he said:

> After prolonged and thorough examination, I have reversed my decision. It no longer seems necessary to me and, therefore, being what I am, I will remain a Jew. But one thing this Yom Kippur has done for me is that it has made me ask myself the question of how much have I grown? How tall can I become spiritually. Every Kol Nidre night for the rest of my life I shall always ask myself that question: How much have I grown, How tall am I spiritually?

I hope that this Yom Kippur and every Yom Kippur, we will continue to ask ourselves, "How much have I grown this year? Have I accepted my destiny as a unique creature of God, or did I flee from my own greatness?"

May our prayers this year and every year fulfill the quest of Rabbi Morris Adler, who said, "Our prayers are answered not when we are given what we ask, but when we are challenged to be what we can be."

May it be Thy will! Amen!

24
Shalom: Wholeness

The famous priestly blessing, birkat kohanim, contains many beautiful thoughts and many important ideas. The climax of the prayer is perhaps the most exhilirating aspect of its fifteen words, *"veyasem l'cha shalom,* may God give you shalom."* Shalom is almost a code word among Jews. We use it to say hello, we use it to say goodbye, we use it for the concept of peace. It appears throughout our Bible, throughout our liturgy—the end of the birkat hamazon, the end of the amidah, other parts of the liturgy. When we see somebody, we sometimes say shalom aleichem, peace, or shalom be unto you.

Shalom is a very difficult word to translate because it has so many different meanings. It has become so popular that it has been accepted even by the non-Jewish world. I am continually amazed when I see the word being accepted today in so many different places.

When Pope Paul visited the Holy Land a number of years ago he greeted those who welcomed him with the word shalom. A Christian group in Pennsylvania that holds retreats

Unedited transcript of tape-recorded talk delivered at Temple Beth El, Rochester, N.Y., May 24, 1975 (Sidra, Naso). Printed in the *Torch,* Spring, 1976.

every weekend at their mountain center, calls their weekend experience a "Shalom Retreat." I have a minister friend in Syracuse who signs every letter, both to me and to everyone else, instead of sincerely, with Shalom followed by his name.

Shalom has become a universal word that has grown out of the Jewish tradition but is not limited to it any more than the Bible or the Ten Commandments, or many other parts of our tradition, have remained only within the precincts of the Jewish people. The word is used in its original because it is so impossible to translate. Remember what the Hebrew poet, Bialik, said about translating—that it's like kissing your lover with a handkerchief between your lips. It's just not the same. You can't get the same flavor of the word. So shalom is an untranslatable concept.

If we want to examine some of the various meanings of the word scientifically, we have to turn to a dictionary which is the classic and most important resource for explaining Hebrew words that are found in the ancient words of the Bible. It is a big volume, about three or four times the size of a Sears catalogue, that we used to refer to in my Seminary days as "B.D.B." If one wants to know the meanings of a Hebrew word in the Bible, he turns to this gigantic book called BDB (for Brown, Driver and Briggs, the three scholars who put together this mammoth scholarly work). This encyclopedia of Jewish etymology of the Bible gives six different interpretations for the word shalom and these are what they are.

First of all, the origin of the word is the Hebrew word shalaim, meaning complete or whole—a sense of totality of unity or wholeness. That's the origin, the real basic fundamental interpretation of the word shalom. In other places in the Bible, the word shalom is used in the sense of safety, soundness, a place where one can be secure to go to. In other biblical passages, in the Psalms, shalom can mean welfare, health or prosperity. In modern Hebrew, if you want to ask someone how he is, you say "Mah shlomcha?," "what is your shalom?" or "what is your health, your welfare, your prosperity?" In still other places in the Bible, a fourth meaning of the word shalom is quiet and tranquillity, a sense of inner contentment, a personal respite from the stirring forces of the outside world.

A fifth of the six meanings in this volume is a trusted friend, an *ish shalom* or *anshei shlomi,* people whom you can rely on, those with whom you are almost bound together with in a kind of pact of trusted friendship. Lastly, the word that we so commonly look upon and use when we think of shalom, is peace, peace from war, peace from international strife, a freedom from conflict.

Yet, if we look at all of these meanings of wholeness, soundness, welfare, tranquillity, trusted friendship and peace, the basic and over-arching significance of this word, even though no one word does sum it all up, is the word *wholeness* because that includes all the other meanings.

When we say shalom means peace that is really not accurate. It is as if we are saying that Washington is identical with the United States—it is only one small part. Some people think peace is identical with shalom, but peace is only one small part of a larger concept of wholeness, of unity, of soundness, togetherness which peace represents.

Since the word shalom is so frequently used in our tradition it really is a summary of what Judaism and what life is supposed to be. If you want to find out about a culture or a civilization, you have to turn to its vocabulary. I am told that the Eskimos have ten or twelve different words for snow. There are so many different kinds and nuances of the word snow that they have to differentiate. Language tells us about the cultural and physical environment, and about the philosophy of a people. The English word charity has something to do with pity, but the Hebrew word for charity is *tzedaka* which means righteousness or obligation which is a different concept of charity, of responsibility. The words of a culture point to the underlying feeling of that culture and civilization.

Therefore, the word shalom is the underlying bedrock foundation of what Judaism tells us about human life and about society and about everything that we do and we think. Life is supposed to have a wholeness, a totality about it, a wholeness and a unity of mind, body, heart, and spirit.

There's an expression in the vernacular that we use today which sums up the word shalom. If you want to describe a person who is doing well emotionally, spiritually and in other ways, you say, he "has it together." A person who has it together is a person who has shalom, who is a whole human being, who is unified, of whom all the parts and pieces are organically connected and function together in a sound and smooth way. Such a person, who has it together, is a person who is a unified and complete, whole human being.

In the passage in Numbers about the Nazir (6:13 ff.), the Nazarite who abstains from strong drink, we find that at the end of his period of nazariteship he has to bring a sin offering. It's very strange why that is the case, because if a person dedicates himself to God he shouldn't have to bring a sin offering. The rabbis ask why is it that he has to bring a sin offering. They say that it is because he refused, even for a short period of time, even in the service of God, to partake of the delights, pleasures, and wonders, the physical pleasures of this universe. So Judaism wants us to be whole people in the sense that we enjoy both body and spirit, both physical and spiritual pleasures. When we abstain from physical pleasure, from drinking wine, we have to bring a sin offering to the temple. This is the first way in which that total human wholeness or soundness comes through in Jewish theology. In

Jewish theology, so many of the dichotomies that exist in other traditions, in other theologies, have no place.

One dichotomy about which so many of us frequently compartmentalize our lives and our thinking is that between science and religion. We say to ourselves that religion deals with the area of emotions, the area of prayer, the area of metaphysics, God and theology, that which cannot be proven, that which is not related to facts, figures and measurements. On the other hand, science is very strictly geared to objectivity, to facts, experimentation, empirical observation of the world. The two realms have no connection whatsoever. One is science and one is religion. But in Judaism we have this concept of wholeness, of soundness, of unity, and science and religion are not two separate realms for us.

When Darwin came along and said that the world was created by evolution and not in the way that the literal interpretation of the Bible seems to explain, that was a great challenge for religionists throughout the world. Science was challenging the fundamental suppositions of religion. But in Judaism that was never the case because we have a great respect for the mind, knowledge, and understanding. It is very easy to mesh and to integrate these various views. We can accept whatever science tells us. There is nothing in Judaism that is irrational or irreasonable or unscientific. Everything really is meta-scientific, if you will, going beyond the facts but not denying or contradicting the facts because life for us is a totality. It is a whole and a unity, and knowledge and objectivity is in no way contradictory with subjectivity, with emotion, with feeling, and with prayer.

Then there is another dichotomy which we frequently hear about between freedom and law.

Judaism is supposed to be a religion of regulation, of laws, of firm, fixed ways of behaving and doing rituals. Those who are so-called free thinkers, or those who believe in following the promptings of their heart, are supposed to be on the other end of the continum and not at all compatible with the sense of law and regimentation of fixed order. In Judaism that is really not the case. For we really have the best of both worlds. There must be spontaneity and a great deal of freedom and individuality. We've never had a catechism, any list of beliefs that you have to accept to be a Jew. We have freedom of thought and even our regimentation, when it comes to ritual and prayer, has a certain amount of freedom in that it helps us to free our spirit and to free our sense of unity with the rest of the world.

One who plays tennis, golf, or baseball knows that if he plays according to the rules and regulations of the game, he is most likely to be free enough to play at his best and to fulfill himself at this sport in the best possible way. Freedom, law, and regularity are not really, in essence, contradictory any more than any other of these dichotomies are contradictory because with us there is shalom, there is wholeness, and there is unity.

For that reason, the unity of the Jewish people has always been so important to us. We have, if you will, denominations as other religions do. There are Orthodox, Conservative, Reform and Reconstructionist, but these really aren't the kind of sharp, clear-cut divisions that they are in other religions. If one is an Episcopalian or a Baptist or a Presbyterian and one wants to change his affiliation, it is almost a matter of conversion from one to the other because these are hard and fast divisions. We Jews, whether we are Sephardic or Ashkenazic, or Reform or Orthodox, whether we are in Israel or in the Diaspora, or whatever the dichotomies among the Jewish people, we're really one large family and these divisions are only in our minds. They are not firm because we consider ourselves all one people.

The same thing goes with the Jewish conception of world peace. The prophets of old, Isaiah, Amos, Micah, dreamed of a world where nations would consider themselves one family— not just our own people—in which all human beings of whatever race, color or creed—would be one whole universe, bound together firmly, as a sound and complete unity. We would never homogenize people to the degree of eliminating differences. We want to retain our individuality, but at the same time we want to bind ourselves in that over-arching unity which is the concept of shalom, of soundness, of wholeness and of peace and prosperity and of totality. That is the ultimate dream of the Jewish tradition, that all men will both be whole and sound within themselves; have it together, if you will. And also have shalom in their relationships with other individuals and with other communities. That we won't look upon others as foreigners, that we won't use those ugly words that we do in war time: Jap, kraut, or names that we used for the Vietnamese, the gooks. These terminologies are totally abhorrent to the concept of shalom, because shalom means the unity of the human family, the soundness of inter-community, of international, of interpersonal, and of intra-psychic relationships, of the wholeness of human life both within us and without us. That, indeed, is a worthy prayer for the ancient priests to have wished upon the worshippers as they came to Jerusalem with their sacrifices. That the Lord will, indeed, bless them and keep them and cause his face to shine upon them and to be gracious to them, but most of all to grant them shalom, to grant them peace, wholeness, soundness.

25
A New Meaning for "Mitzvah"

In this brief essay, I would like to suggest a new way of understanding the ancient Hebrew value-concept of *mitzvah*. Traditionally, the word of God, the command or direction from Heaven, mitzvah, is an act or deed which is required by God of those who would be His chosen people, and fulfill the mandates of His sacred covenant.

For moderns who have difficulty accepting the simplistic notion that God transmitted "commands" or specific directions to man, it is necessary to closely examine this notion of mitzvah. It is obviously a crucial element in Jewish religious faith and observance and, in fact, the major differentiating factor in American Jewish denominations. Not to be able to accept it in its full traditional understanding need not necessitate eliminating the entire notion of mitzvah. Indeed, elimination of this key value-concept in Judaism would leave a cultural-religious heritage which is denuded of one of its core concepts and key identifying principles.

Already Borowitz and other "Covenant theologians" have discussed mitzvah in terms of an opportunity to meet God, a dialogic moment of encounter with the Almighty which creates a unique existential opportunity for meeting/feeling our Maker. This is a far cry from the traditional conception of a Heavenly direction, a deed to be performed for the sake of upholding a divine-human agreement. Yet it preserves the key element of mitzvah, namely, the opportunity to experience God's will, to carry out the wishes of God, though in a more generalized way than merely doing a ritual.

THE VIEW OF HUMANISTIC PSYCHOLOGY

A new conception of mitzvah grows out of the writings of Abraham Maslow, whose own Jewish upbringing, while stultifying and oppressive, seems to have influenced his writings on the need for value-oriented understanding of human behavior.

According to Maslow, human motivation derives from a hierarchy of needs, starting with basic physiological needs, moving to needs for security and safety, then to belongingness and love, to esteem and finally for self-actualization. Lower needs (physiological, security needs) are prepotent or they require fulfillment before the higher needs can be felt and realized. However, the needs for love and recognition are just as important to human fulfillment as the need for food, sunlight, and calcium. Going further, the need for self-actualization, a value-oriented life of meaning, purpose and ultimate fulfillment, is in the very same category as previous needs in the hierarchy.

In other words, "the state of being without a system of values is psychopathogenic" or productive of value-illness. This illness is referred to by Maslow as "apathy, amorality, hopelessness, cynicism." "The human being needs a frame-work of values, a philosophy of life, a religion or religion-

surrogate to live by and understand by, in the same sense that
he needs sunlight, calcium, or love."

Maslow distinguishes between D-needs and B-needs
(Deficiency needs and Being needs, the latter often called
"growth needs"). Deficiency needs are created when the lower
levels of needs in the need hierarchy are not met, such as
physiological, safety, love and esteem. Emotional illness is
caused by the failure to meet these needs. Therapy consists in
filling them. But then there are higher needs, growth needs, or
meta-needs, which are needs for the values of self-actualization. These include needs for such values as truth, goodness,
beauty, aliveness, individuality, completion, justice, order,
richness, playfulness, self-sufficiency, and meaningfulness.

Previous understandings of the nature of man have
focused on the unconscious layers of personality (psychoanalysis) and the response to outside stimuli (behaviorism).
These systems recognized human motives as growing out of
the need to avoid or escape pain and discomfort. Beside these
self-protective motives, Maslow posits higher motives, which
are equally important in understanding human behavior. The
higher motives for truth, goodness, beauty, and justice are
just as important as the lower ones. Without them, man
cannot be healthy and fulfilled.

The purpose of mitzvah traditionally has been to help
man achieve fulfillment, to find health, morality and normal-
ity through obedience to God's will. A modern understanding
of God's will is that there is a divine urge for man to be
healthy, fulfilled, and fulfill his innermost need for values and
full humaness (self-actualization).

Mitzvah, then, is the fulfillment of the growth needs, the
health needs, the higher needs (B-needs). Mitzvah is an act
which responds to God's will that man find truth, goodness,
beauty, and justice. Through humanistic psychology, or more
accurately, through modern man's recognition of a new and

higher need that helps us better understand human behavior at its best and noblest, we have discovered God's purpose and design in creating man. Man needs truth, goodness, justice, and beauty the very same way he needs calcium and vitamins. Their absence is illness-producing and their presence is illness-preventing. Mitzvah is the act which reflects growth motivation. It is the deed which brings fulfillment of the divinely-ordained needs of man for a value-oriented life.

If it be God's will that man find order, individuality, richness, meaningfulness, and other values of self-actualization, then man fulfills God's will by acting in ways that bring these values into his life and into society. Such a way of acting can be justifiably termed performing mitzvot. A person does a mitzvah when he helps himself and others to become fuller, healthier people who aspire to the fulfillment of man's highest and noblest needs. Performing a mitzvah is then being faithful to God's covenant, acting in agreement with His design in creation, and answering a call from the Deity which is built into the very life of man's biological/spiritual nature.

Observing Shabbat, honoring parents, loving one's neighbor, lighting the Menorah, having equal scales, shaking lulav and etrog, and caring for the stranger, are all acts which bring out the highest nature of man and fulfill the highest motivating needs (growth needs) of human behavior. They help to foster truth, goodness, beauty, order and meaningfulness. They are God's desire, His way for man to perfect the world as well as himself. They are, thus, mitzvot.

26
How God Talks to Us Today

From time to time, I like to invite some of the classes of my Religious School into my study and have a conversation with them. We share some candy together, sit around and chat, and then they are allowed to ask any question that they like, either stemming from their religious studies, school, class, something that has a connection with a Jewish holiday or observance, ritual, or whatever. Interestingly enough, many of the questions that I receive have to do with questions of theology. Starting with the youngest of the children, they being to think for themselves about the meaning, not only of the content, but of the concepts of the Bible, the siddur, of God and the eternal questions that bother adults as well as children.

The one question that I seem to receive most frequently has to do with the revelation of God to man. Children don't phrase it in those terms. They probably never even heard the word *revelation*. The children phrase it in a very simple way, but the question is very profound. That is, why doesn't God speak to the people today as He did to Moses, as He did to others in the days of the Bible? It's a very simple, logical

Published in the *Jewish Spectator,* Spring, 1976.

question to young minds as they read the words of the stories of how God appeared to man, Moses especially, and spoke to him the words of the laws, customs, traditions, ideals of Judaism. Why doesn't God speak today to us the way he did in the days of the Bible? After discussing the issue in the most simple and direct terms that I can, the ultimate conclusions we always come to in our discussions is that in a very real sense, God *does* speak to man today even as He did in the days of the Bible and that God does reveal His will and His spirit, His faith, as it were, as He did in the days of Moses at Mt. Sinai.

Theologians today refer to this viewpoint of Conservative and Reform Judaism as "progressive revelation." That is, that God did not only reveal His will in ancient times, but has continued to reveal Himself, throughout every generation, to leaders, to great men and women, to great spirits of the age, who received that vision. In his own way, each individual, in his own expression, in his own symbolism, hearing, feeling, receives the communication of God.

I would like to share some very personal views on how God does reveal His will and how God does communicate to persons in this world, the Twentieth Century. Even in modern technological society, I think we can see the evidence of this special revelation of God's will in the instances of our daily lives. These are personal views and I am sure you have your own instances and your own thoughts and feelings about how God seems to enter people's lives in various ways. The ways are there, but we don't always see them.

The first way in which I feel God's disclosing presence is in the realm of prayer. When the words are recited, chanted, and people sway and they hum and they daven, this can be and very often is a revelation of the feeling of the presence and spirit of God within man. Or sometimes it doesn't have to be the chanting of the ancient Hebrew melodies but a meaningful English prayer with certain words or phrases or ideas that strike our heart. I think that people feel the sense of God in their lives. I think there are certain sights, certain visions which bring us the feeling that God is more closely present disclosing himself to us.

One of the sights that moves me personally is the sanctuary of my own Temple. As I worship there every week and particularly as I look at the ten windows representing the Ten Commandments of the original revelaton of God's will, and see the lights and the various strengths of their brightness flow in from the outside world into the sanctuary and paint their multi-colored visions upon the red bricks of the sanctuary, it is as if God Himself were entering with a large hand and a brush and colors, painting the walls with His ideas, His words, and His presence.

I think the vision of seeing someone in a talit, or tefillin is to me an occasion when I see the very special presence of God. Or when, in my memory, I look back on the years when I was in Camp Ramah as a counselor and the beautiful Friday night service when all of the participants were dressed in white, sitting out in the open, with the trees and the beauty of nature surrounding us, and the stirring words of the Kabbalat Shabbat service, this too was an experience of God's divine presence emerging into man and the universe.

I particularly find the sense of God when I am surrounded by Judaism in its hasidic expression, whether it be the hasidic garb, the music, the dance, the spirit, or whatever it might be—it seems that the hasidic Jews capture the spirit of God's self-disclosure so much more intensely than the rest of us can. When I see hasidim or when I feel or hear the words of their songs, I, too, try to capture the spirit of God disclosing Himself to man.

Then there are special days, such as Yom Kippur and the Avodah Service when we read about the Kohain Gadol going into the Holy of Holies, that one special moment of the entire year. Or when we read the martyrology, the Eleh Ezkarah, or the Kol Nidre, or other special moments that help us to feel God's presence in our prayer and in our worship. The first category, then, of feeling God's presence, is in the category of worship and prayer.

Another category would be that of intimate, personal relationships. In these relationships, I see and feel the special presence of God helping man relate to man, helping a person to become closer to another human being. In that experience, in that personal expression, I feel there is an element of divinity, whether it be an encounter group, or a sensitivity group at one extreme, or just merely a youth group discussion, or teaching a class, or sitting around a dinner table with a few very close friends—these are the various ways in which men and women intimately relate one to another. It seems that the presence of God is there in a more special sense than in other occasions.

A third area for me has to do with my professional life and I am sure others in their own lives can relate similar instances. When I sit down at my typewriter to write a sermon or an article, or whatever it might be, I feel that special aura of God's presence as I see the words and ideas fall right out on the page. There seems to be some special, non-human contribution or participation that symbolizes, for me, God's presence. It could be the surgeon at the moment he is repairing the body of another human being, or the lawyer defending a client in the courtroom, or a carpenter finishing a beautiful piece of work, or a plumber repairing some household fixtures. Whatever it might be, each of us, in his own way, as we see our work completed and as we see that which we were trained for coming into wholeness and completion, the special presence of God making our universe one and creative seems to fall into place.

Another area, for me, of God's revelation, is that of

walking. One of the most delightful things and one of the most delightful ways for me to feel God's presence is walking to or from the synagogue, or walking through a park or a field, or walking in a special place, such as the city of Jerusalem. These are some of the experiences of God-moments for me. When the weather is nice and the sun is shining, or when I see young people dancing, especially Israeli folk dances, it is the same kind of feeling.

In other areas, when I hear stories of kindness of one human being toward another, these to me are God's disclosing of Himself in the lives of human beings. When I hear about our synagogue groups working to integrate the Soviet Jews in our city and to the life of the Jewish community, welcoming them, being hospitable to them. When I hear that some of my congregation visited the Jewish Home for the Aged or when I read the story of the Book of Ruth and hear how this Gentile woman accepted the religion of her mother-in-law and Ruth clung to Naomi and became a support and a friend and developed a very intimate and loving relationship with her, these acts of kindness, these acts of altruism, are times when God reveals Himself in our Lives.

One more very important time when I feel God's presence is when I am standing under the Hupah facing a young bride and groom. I look into their eyes and as they look at each other, see the love and the special wonder of that relationship, as they clasp each other's hands so tightly at this sacred moment to them. To me that is a time when God is revealing Himself to humankind.

Lastly, I would say when I have the great opportunity of studying Torah. When I read the words of the Psalms, of the Siddur, of Rashi's commentaries, or the theology of Rabbi Heschel, or the poetry of Yehuda HaLevy, or a story by Sholom Aleichem or some hasidic rabbi, or a biography of a great Jew, or other human being—all of this to me, when I participate in this experience of sharing the culture and the vision and the feeling of other people in the written word, that to me is an experience when God shows Himself to man. When man is functioning at his highest, striving to become better, to reach out and to receive those two tablets, to know how best to live one's life and to reach the true fulfillment for which a human being was created, such a moment to me is a God-moment.

A hasidic rabbi tells us that Shavuot is called *z'man matan torateinu*—the time of the giving of the Torah. It was given this name, rather than *z'man kabbalat torateinu,* the time of the receiving of the Torah, because the Torah was given only once—but it is received in every generation. The receiving of the Torah depends upon each individual human being, whether or not he individually, as a person, is ready and prepared to receive the Torah. *Z'man matan torateinu* is the time when we remember how the Torah was given. But each day, in every way, in our own lives we have the opportunity to create our own festival of *z'man kabbalat torateinu,* the receiving, the being open to the disclosure of God's will in our lives. If we open ourselves to these divine moments of human life, if we feel that special presence of divinity surrounding us, enveloping us, and filling us inside and outside, if we can do this—receive the Torah, as Moses received it in his day, then we shall surely be observing all of Judaism and all of life in the spirit with which our tradition commands us.

27
Meditation is
Transcendentally Jewish

There are two basic genres of meditation. Western meditation involves a head-trip in which the meditator is lost in thought and cogitation. Eastern meditation signifies a calm and passive state in which thoughts are allowed to pass quietly without comment and analysis so that the mind can reach deep down into its alpha zones.

It is my contention that both kinds of meditation are Jewish. Basing themselves on Genesis 24:63, the rabbis claim that Isaac created the *mincha* service. "Isaac went out to meditate in the field." Surely this was to daven mincha, argues the Talmud. Knowing that mincha was the product of a much later age, the ancient sages ascribed *mincha* to Isaac because they needed to give it the authority of age and the prestige of the Torah. But Isaac was a spiritual figure, and afternoon prayer was not out of keeping with his basic nature. It was ok to say that Isaac wrote *mincha,* because there is nothing new under the sun and all new things are built upon old foundations. Why not, then, legitimize modern techniques of meditation, of Eastern and Western bents, by finding

Published in the Jewish Spectator, Summer, 1975.

antecedents in traditional literature? The rabbis did it and so can we!

The Mishna (Berachot 5:1) informs us that "The pious men of old used to wait an hour before beginning to recite their prayers in order to concentrate their thoughts upon the Omnipresent." In his commentary on the Mishna, Maimonides (12th century) explains: "This means that they would delay their prayers one hour in order to *relax their mind,* and to *quiet their thoughts,* and then they were ready to pray."

What Maimonides wrote in the twelfth century is not far from the description of those promoting Transcendental Meditation, or Eastern meditation. Our mind, they tell us, is like an active machine, constantly thinking, racing its wheels, grinding frantically. We need to "quiet our thoughts" and "relax our minds", to use Maimonides' words, before going out into life.

Dr. Edward W. Maupin, of the Esalen Institute in California, writes that meditation is "a clear, relaxed awareness in which the flow of thought is reduced and an attitude of detached observation is maintained. In contrast to the usual thinking activity, which carries one off into abstractions or fantasies, this observing attitude keeps close contact with the here-and-now experience. Thoughts are not prevented but are allowed to pass without elaboration" (*Ways of Growth,* edited by Herbert Otto and John Mann, page 205).

In today's frantically paced society, we find many symptoms of spiritual malaise. Physical manifestations include heart attacks, ulcers, high blood pressure, skin rashes. Psychological symptoms include increasing divorce rates, family breakdown, job failure, neurosis, and psychosis. The message of Judaism is that the heart of life is the inner world, the life of the spirit. Shabbat, festivals, daily prayer, teshuva, and fasting are all methods at helping us get a new perspective on life, methods of growth. Meditation is another arrow in the spiritual quiver.

In the brochure distributed by the International Meditation Society one finds goals totally compatible with Judaism's attitudes: "After meditating, an individual naturally engages in activity more effectively without accumulating stress and strain. With expanded awareness, increased clarity of perception and more profound knowledge of life, he acts in a more loving and creatively intelligent manner. Transcendental Meditation unfolds the full potential of his mind and heart, making life a joy both for himself and others."

It is easy to be skeptical after hearing such dramatic claims. But more and more intelligent people in all walks of life, Jews and Gentiles, are meditating. Transcendental Meditation is a technique and not a creed. It therefore is not, or should not be, threatening to adherents of any traditional faith. Teachers in public and private schools are receiving in-service credit for taking courses in meditation. Leaders in science, industry, sports, as well as airplane pilots, musicians, and prison inmates are meditating with many positive benefits. They report a more relaxed awareness of life, deeper contact with their inner resources, greater ability to cope with stress, improved body functioning, and a greater feeling of vitality and spirituality.

Dr. Sidney Jourard, of the University of Florida, states in his book, *Healthy Personality* (Macmillan, page 300), "Meditation is a way of leaving or transcending one's everyday situation, in order to get perspective upon one's life, and to see new possibilities in stagnant situations . . . Meditation is . . . a valid approach to personal growth and a meaningful way to spend leisure time."

The Hasidim knew of the importance of meditation to the life of the spirit. In Rabbi Heschel's posthumous book, *A Passion for Truth,* he wrote: "Hasidic lore tells us that as a young man the Baal Shem Tov spent many years alone in the Carpathian Mountains.

"Solitude was a common practice among mystically inclined Jews. Even the non-mystical Jewish writers of the Middle Ages seemed to agree that solitary living was indispensable to the attainment of spiritual purity.

"According to . . . Reb Naham of Bratslav, solitude is an indispensable prerequisite for spiritual living. He called upon his disciples to set aside an hour or more every day for seclusion and meditation, whether in an isolated room or in the fields" (page 215).

Is it so far-fetched, then, to say, with the rabbis, that Abraham, who first envisioned one God, and who often sat at the door of his tent, created Yoga; that Isaac, who meditated often in the field, founded transcendental meditation; and that Jacob, who wrestled with the angel, fell upon rolfing and bio-energetics?

28
The Spiritual Element

When Moses began to feel the heavy load of responsibility for his large hord of former slaves, he asked God to help and God replied by asking Moses to select seventy leaders to assist him. Moses was told that God would then take of Moses' spirit and transfer it to these newly-ordained leaders.

The Talmudic rabbis ask an obvious question: When God takes of Moses' spirit to give it to the elders, does he thereby diminish that of Moses? What effect does this giving of prophetic power to the seventy assistants have on the original leader?

As with so many things, the ancient rabbis answered with a simile. Leadership, prophecy, spirituality, they declared, is like a candle. When its light, energy, is given over to another, its glow remains strong. It is not reduced one whit through the process of sharing. Similarly, Moses' own strength and authority, his ability to inspire and excite the masses, is not at all diminshed through sharing his spirit with the seventy elders.

Another powerful Talmudic illustration carries the same message. Two merchants were conversing one afternoon in the

Delivered at Temple Beth El, Rochester, N.Y., May 31, 1975 (Be-haalote-kha)

224

marketplace when trade was slow. One said to the other: "I sell linen and you sell vegetables. Why not take some of my merchandise and I'll take some of yours. We'll both benefit." They did so, and then the other merchant initiated this conversation: "What did we gain by this transaction? We each received something new, but we each paid a price for it. We lost something from our own stock. However, let's do the following. I studied a chapter of Bible this morning and so did you. I'll teach you my chapter and you teach me yours. Then both of us will have gained without having lost anything at all."

The lesson is the same. When spiritual things are transferred, they do not require a loss in kind, as in barter and trade of material things. In fact, this is but one instance of several ways in which the laws of the material world and those of the spiritual world differ. Another way is the size of their influence in comparison with things which take up space. Things of the spirit have an influence far out of proportion to their size. Material things are forceful in terms of their size. An idea that is powerful can be expressed in a brief phrase, yet it may be able to move mountains.

Another difference between matter and spirit is that intangible gifts, such as love, friendship, knowledge, and charisma can be in many places at once. A chair, a table, a book, a person, can only be in one place at one time. Not so an idea, a theory, a feeling, a memory. They can be in many places simultaneously.

Still another distinction between things physical and things spiritual is that the former lose their vitality as time passes. A building, an automobile, a person becomes weaker after a certain length of existence. "Nothing lasts forever" is a truism. Yet, an idea, a truth, a poem, gets more powerful with time. Rather than shrinking its reach, it extends it. It does not function according to the laws of the physical world.

Recognizing these important differences between the realm of the spirit and the realm of material things, it seems that we should be devoting at least equal energy, time and resources—our own and the world's—to developing our inner side. But, alas, it is not so! Teilhard de Chardin reminds us that the real task of our century, after we have mastered the winds and the tides, is to generate the capacity of human beings to love one another. When we can achieve that we shall again have discovered fire, said the late Catholic sage. Or as William Morrow put it, "What lies behind us and what lies before us are tiny matters compared to what lies within us."

I often wonder what the results would be if people were to study the proportion of time they spend on just surviving—earning a living, acquiring material goods, striving for comfort and security, caring for the bodily needs, building and repairing homes and stocking them with as many creature-comforts as we can. It would, I dare say, probably be in the high 80s or 90s. The percentage of our lives given over to things of the spirit, wherein nature's laws operate in a far more ennobling way, is pitifully miniscule.

It is probably true that for most people the things which matter the most are given the least attention. The cultivation of our minds, the sensitization of our hearts, the training of our eyes and ears, all take second place to the strengthening of our capacity to earn and achieve power and wealth. The capacity to yearn, to sing, to hope, to dream, are given short shrift by the energy given over to achieving the maintenance tasks of life.

A story reported recently in the Rochester (New York) *Democrat and Chronicle* touched me deeply. Dr. M. Richard Rose, president of Alfred University, wrote of a time when he was employed by the Defense Department. Working for him was a former soldier named Nick, who was taken captive in the Delta Region of South Vietnam while leading a five-man patrol. "The first morning after their capture, some makeshift bamboo cages were brought out and lined up in the compound and they were asked to confess to germicidal warfare.

"Upon refusing to confess, one member of the patrol was shot and his body was left to lie in the sun throughout the day. The ritual was repeated the following morning and for three successive days . . . .

"The next morning a raid on the Viet Cong encampment caused the Viet Cong to scatter and flee. Nick was rushed off and he never saw another American for four and a half years. He spent most of his time in a bamboo cage, but he kept himself alive mentally with a very active imagination.

"Few of us will ever be tested in such a dramatic fashion, yet I feel the limiting factor in the lives of all too many people is the lack of attention to a spritual belief, to the development of our emotions and a childlike awe and wonderment about the world around us . . . .

"The individuals who have contributed most are those whose values were centered on truth and beauty and reason. A personal value system is absolutely necessary today if we are going to derive full satisfaction from living."

Another tale comes to mind in this connection. A man was speeding down a highway, when the siren of a motorcycle stopped him. The policeman asked the driver a number of pointed questions. "Did you notice the bed of tulips on a lovely green patch dividing the highway about five miles back?" he queried. "No," replied the driver.

"What about the purple flowers planted a few yards from the road about three miles back?" Again, a *no* answer.

"Did you see the magnificent aqueduct and waterfalls on the left side of the road just beyond the bend in the road?"

"No, sir, I did not."

Finally, the policeman came in for the attack. "Look here, pal, our government spends alot of dollars making this roadway beautiful and pleasant and interesting. Why rush past it all and miss it?"

How many of us race down the highway of life without paying attention to the beauty and the pleasantness on the right and the left? How many of us are so preoccupied with "making it" that we never get to appreciate it once we've made it? How many people die after lives of quiet desperation, after having waited too long for the day wherein they would be able to start appreciating art and poetry and sailing and loving? How many of us are in such a hurry to get where we're going, that we forget why we're travelling?

In this frenetic rush to arrive, to succeed, we lose our souls, we crush our spirits, we stifle our inner life. Our hands are too tense to let go and open our eyes to our own beauty and that of those closest to us.

Friends, it is the travelling that provides the greatest opportunity to find spirit. The beauty and grandeur of the human spirit is not to be found at the end of life only, but mostly in the abundance of years along the way.

Let us all begin to measure more closely the precious hours and minutes we fritter away on inanities, and begin to maximize the use of the days we have to cultivate our deepest core of personhood. This will take more reflection, more examination, more evaluation, more opportunity for what the late Rabbi Heschel called "radical amazement" and awesome wonder. It will mean giving the highest priority to those areas of our personal development which operate on laws which are far different and far more ennobling spiritually from the norms of physics and geometry.

The prophet Zechariah said it in these words: "'Not by might, nor by power, but by My spirit,' saith the Lord of hosts."

29
Two Kinds of Darkness

The Bible describes the plague of darkness, the ninth plague, in the following words:

> The Lord said to Moses: Hold out your arm toward the sky that there may be darkness upon the land of Egypt, a darkness that can be felt. Moses held out his arm toward the sky and thick darkness descended upon all the land of Egypt for three days. People could not see one another, and for three days no one could get up from where he was; but all the Israelites enjoyed light in their dwellings. (Exodus 10:21-23)

The Bible speaks, of course, of literal darkness, in which no one could find his way through the homes and pathways of Egypt. But there is another kind of darkness with which Egypt was plagued, a spiritual darkness. In Egypt, "people could not see one another," and thus there was the darkness of the heart, of the spirit, as well as of the eye.

The Egyptian people were plagued by a society that relied on slaves for building its mammoth pyramids; a society which cruelly oppressed foreigners and strangers; a society enslaved to a concept of after-life that so pre-occupied its members with

Delivered at Temple Beth El, Rochester, January 26, 1974 (Sidra Bo)

material comforts in the next world that they could not pay attention to the legitimate needs of this world. It was thus a society that was cruel and bigoted and oppressive.

Various commentators describe the bigotry and oppression of Egyptian society, based on the words of the three verses quoted earlier, exposing the rank inequities and gross injustices in Egyptian life. Let us examine the biblical verses and their explanations.

First, the Torah tells us that the darkness of Egypt was a thick, palpable darkness, "ve-yamesh choshekh," "darkness which may be felt." (Exodus 10:21)

The Midrash explains that the darkness which enveloped Egypt was as thick as a golden *denar.* The pursuit of the grandeur and splendor of a sparkling materialistic civilization made Egyptian people greedy for an abundance of luxuries and comforts, for themselves, but not for the poor, the orphan, the stranger.

This is an affliction that many societies face, including our own. Our reliance is upon gold, rather than upon the golden rule. We cannot manage our lives without a superabundance of material possessions. We fritter away our precious hours in amassing material goods, to the exclusion of time for family, for prayer, for study.

A Hasidic rebbe once took his pupil, a wealthy miser, to the window of his living room, and asked him to look out. "What do you see," asked the master. "People," replied the rich pupil. Next the rebbe took his student to a mirror, with the same question: "What do you see?" "Myself," came the reply. "You see," explained the teacher, "both the window and the mirror are made of glass. Yet the mirror is covered with silver. As soon as the silver is added, you stop seeing others and can only see yourself."

The people of Egypt were so greedy that their lives were void of the light of compassion and concern, and enveloped only in the darkness of greed. "Money buys everything," wrote Carl Sandburg, "except love, personality, freedom, immortality, silence, and peace."

Rudyard Kipling once advised a graduating class at McGill University, not to care too much for money or power or fame, for "someday you will meet a man who cares for none of these things. . .and then you will know how poor you are. . . ."

The second thing the Torah says about the darkness in Egypt is this: "Lo ra-u eesh et achiv," "People could not see one another." (Exodus 10:23)

The only thing worse than being immune to the needs and concerns of those around us is death. An uncaring life is almost as bad as, or perhaps worse than, death. It has been said that "a man wrapped up in himself makes a very small package." Judaism's golden rule is "Love your neighbor as yourself." If one's heart and mind are blinded by spiritual darkness, making it impossible to feel and see the hurts of his neighbor, then the most important rule in Jewish tradition is violated.

With the onset of Daylight Saving Time religious Jews had the problem of knowing when to recite the Shma and other morning prayers. Most people leave for work now before it is light out. In the Talmud there is a debate about the permissible time to recite the morning Shma. When does night technically end and day officially begin? One rabbi said: "The night ends and a new day begins when you can tell the difference between a blue thread and a purple thread." Another rabbi suggests: "The night ends and the day begins when you can see the face of your brother."

It is seeing the face of our brothers and sisters that marks the dawn of day. Only those wishing to live through a dark and black night of selfishness will not strive to seek out the face of his brother. According to Jonathan Swift, "There's none so blind as they that won't see." The prophet Jeremiah upbraids his flock in these words: "Hear this, O foolish and senseless people, who have eyes, but see not, who have ears, but hear not" (5:21).

Helen Keller, who spent most of her life without physical sight, described darkness in these words:

> I have walked with people whose eyes are full of light but who see nothing in sea or sky, nothing in city streets, nothing in books. It were far better to sail forever in the night of blindness with sense, and feeling, and mind, than to be content with the mere act of seeing. The only lightless dark is the night of darkness in ignorance and insensibility.

The third thing the Torah tells us about the darkness of Egypt is "ve-lo kamu eesh mee-tachtav," "No one could get up from where he was" (Exodus 10:23).

Not only could no one rise from his place because of the physical darkness, but no one could grow to become a better person. No one could reach beyond the place, the level, at which his personality and character were immovably fixed. Egyptian society was not a growing society, not a dynamic, searching society, but rather it was made up of small people who remained the same size throughout their lives. Their spiritual growth was stunted. Each day and each month failed to bring anything new to them in the way of knowledge, appreciation, sensitivity. There was no psychological nor intellectual growth in the darkness of Egyptian society. "Lo kamu eesh mee-tachtav," no one arose from his lower self to his higher, better, self. No one in Egypt expressed the thought found in Lord Tennyson's prayer:

Ah for a man to arise in me,
That the man that I am
May cease to be

A Roman once asked the ancient sage, Rabbi Akiba: Why did not God make man precisely as He wanted him to be? The sage answered: Because it is man's obligation to perfect himself, to rise above his lower self, and reach higher and higher towards the level of his best self.

Once long ago a subject appeared before the famous King, Alexander the Great, who ruled the ancient world in the fourth century B.C.E. Alexander was judging a defendant standing before him, and found him guilty, sentencing him to death. "I appeal," protested the subject. "To whom?" answered the great King. "There is no authority higher than myself." "Your majesty," proclaimed the condemned victim, "I appeal from Alexander the Small to Alexander the Great."

A society which does not, through its history, its traditions, its laws, its ideals, appeal to its members from their smaller selves to their higher selves, is indeed enveloped in the worst kind of darkness. Chesterton once wrote, "If seed in the black earth can turn into such beautiful roses, what might not the heart of man become in its long journey toward the stars?" Egyptian society was plagued with a dearth of people travelling toward the stars. "Lo kamu eesh mee-tachtav." No one rose up from his present stature to achieve better and nobler things.

Interestingly enough, the Bible concludes the description of the ninth plague by telling us: "ule-chol bnai yisrael haya or bemoshvotam," "But all the Israelites enjoyed light in their dwellings" (Exodus 10:23).

Was ancient Israel able to survive the darkness because there was physical light in their dwelling places? I wonder. Or was it that despite the darkness of the surrounding culture, despite the selfishness, the greed, the narrowness, the oppression, the absence of spiritual and intellectual growth, the Israelites had a patriarchal tradition which demanded justice, kindness, truth, and freedom? Torah Orah! Light is Torah, Light is knowledge! Light is growth and enlightenment!

In the prayer we recite each Saturday night to usher out the Shabbat, we say these words: "La-yehudim hayta ora ve-simcha vesason veekar," "The Jewish people have always been privileged to have light and joy and gladness and honor." The prayer then continues: "ken tihyeh lanu!" "May it always be so with us!" Amen.

30
Humanizing Death

The subject of death and dying is a complex, mysterious and complicated subject which covers a great many themes. I, therefore, want to limit myself to three general areas. What is Judaism's attitude toward death?, Judaism's method of gradual return to normalcy through its series of grief rituals, and lastly, the view that the end of a person's life should have as much dignity, as much peacefulness as possible.

First of all, death as a reality of life. I think that's the way Judaism looks at death. We all think we are immortal; we are just never going to die. I remember reading a letter a number of years ago from a soldier in Vietnam who was killed soon after writing the letter. He wrote the letter to his father, saying that he and his friends take all the risks in the world because they feel themselves immortal—nothing could ever possibly happen to them. Something did. We take foolish risks sometimes—we don't fasten our safety belts, we smoke too much, we don't watch our eating habits, we don't exercise. We don't take care of ourselves, we don't think about these things because after all, we are immortal. Nobody really is prepared to admit to himself that life is finite.

Unedited transcription from a tape recording of a lecture delivered to the Sisterhood of Temple Beth El, December 6, 1973. This essay was co-recipient of the Hyman G. Enelow Award of the Jewish Theological Seminary, May, 1976.

Death holds for us a tremendous sense of terror, fear, and anxiety. It is very difficult for most people to talk about death. Since we can't talk about it, and we can't admit to ourselves that some day we are going to die, all of us, we repress those feelings, about death, we deny them, by saying we are immortal, it will never happen to me.

Of course we move in and out of periods of reality and unreality, of admission and of repression, of admission and denial, but there is a very strong sub-conscious attempt on the part of the human psyche to deny it all in order to keep us stable and happy. If we thought about our death all the time we wouldn't be very happy, normal people. We would be morbid. To prevent ourselves from becoming morbid we have a necessary mechanism within us that represses, that denies, pushes it out of our mind. While it is a necessary aspect of our psyche, sometimes it is abused like everything else and there has to be a way to deal with it.

Denial is expressed in many ways. For example through the many euphemisms we employ. We don't say a person dies. When we call someone to transmit the tragic news, we don't say Mr. Cohen died. We say, he expired, passed away. From the pulpit we say, departed, gathered unto his fathers. The word *death* is a fearful word. Part of our denial, our repression, is avoiding its use.

In an article published by a prominent anthropologist a number of years ago, the author pointed out that there is a kind of pornography of death today. We try so much to deny and to repress. Just as in Victorian times sex was taboo, today death is taboo. We don't want to talk about it. That's a kind of pornography of death.

In previous times, people used to die at home, before all the medical advances and sophisticated hospitals and old age homes, and the child would see his grandfather die. He would see the doctor come in the last stages of his illness and he would get the feeling from the family that something terrible was about to happen. It would be part of life. It would be one of the things he remembers out of his childhood—part of life just as everything else is. It is one of the stages of passage just as birth. A child witnesses his brother's *bris* (ritual circumcision) or his sister's naming, or his brother's bar mitzvah or his own, or weddings, funerals. Death was a natural part of life. Today it is much more hidden; we don't see people die. We are not with them when they die. Even adults are very rarely with anyone who has died. Very rarely have we seen anyone who is dead. This is all part of the 20th century hiding and repressing death. One child was told (typical of the TV generation) that her grandfather had died. She responded by saying, who shot him? This is the only way that children know about death—from what they see on the television, cowboys and Indians.

When the life insurance man comes to the house, the wife will quickly disappear into the other room. She doesn't want to talk about her husband's death. It is too fearful: let him worry about those things. Then when it comes to the funeral ceremonies in the larger cities there are elaborate funerals. There is beautiful music and flowers all over, an open casket, and it is very much like a farewell party. The body is beautified and decorated, all kinds of make-up is used (just as in Hollywood) to make a person as beautiful, as wonderful as he or she could possibly look. It is a kind of display, an exhibit, like a museum. That helps us to really think, if we want to be unrealistic, that the person is not really dead. He/she is merely sleeping and will sleep that way forever. The lovely coffin with the padded linen interior, sometimes even a lovely mausoleum, is a new home for the person while he sleeps. It is very easy for us to say they are not really dead. There is no such thing as death. We are all immortal. Sometimes the denial is a necessary aspect of our reaction and it should be. As I said, we can't be morbid about it, we cannot let our mind dwell upon it. When we first hear about death, we say to ourselves immediately, it's not true. It didn't happen. You can't adjust to it. I'm usually the first one to visit a bereaved family. The first reaction constantly is: "I just don't believe it's true. This morning we sat down and had a cup of coffee together and now he's not here any more. I can't believe it." That's part of the healthy mechanism of gradual adjustment. But ultimately that has to give way to a sense of reality. I remember when I heard that President Kennedy was shot, my first reaction was—oh, he was shot in the arm. They'll take him to the hospital and he'll be better. The President isn't going to die. Everything is all right. We all probably thought the same thing. But, it's not true. Like the husband who once said to the wife: If one of us dies, I'll go to Paris. There is no such thing as death. The psychologist Rollo May said that the repression of death is "what makes modern life banal, empty, vapid. We run away from death by making a cult of automatic progress, or making it impersonal. Many people think they are facing death when they are really side-stepping it with the old eat drink and be merry for tomorrow you die." Middle-aged men and women who want to love everybody, go every place, do everything, hear everything before the end comes. Like the advertising slogan, "if I've only one life, let me live it as a blond."

Yet, Judaism stresses the reality of death. It helps us to overcome this repression and denial which initially may be healthy but if persistent can be dangerous because it is not true, it is a falsehood, it is a cover-up, it is unhealthy. There is a very lovely passage which I almost invariably read at a funeral before the eulogy, written by the ancient sage Ben Sira, who wrote the book, the Wisdom of Ben Sira. It is not in the Bible, it is one of the books excluded from the Bible (Apocrypha) but a Jewish book nevertheless, from the fourth century B.C.E. Even then Judaism had this realistic attitude towards death. "Fear not death for we are destined to die. We share it with all who ever lived, with all who ever will be. Bewail the dead, hide not your grief. Do not restrain your mourning but remember that continuing sorrow is worse than death. When the dead are at rest, let their memory rest and be consoled when the soul departs."

That's reality. We're *all* going to die. We have to accept it. That's what Ben Sira is trying to say. The same concept is found in the Bible. In the ninetieth Psalm, which is also sometimes read at funerals: "Man you crumble to dust. You say, return O mortals. A thousand years in your sight are as a passing day, an hour of night. You sweep men away and they sleep. Like grass they flourish but for a day. In the morning they sprout afresh, by nightfall, they fade and wither. Three score and ten our years may number. Four score years if granted with vigor, laden with travail and trouble. Life quickly passes away, and flies away." Life is finite. We have to accept that.

Judaism insists further that the coffin be closed during and before funeral services. This is not a person anymore. It is merely a body. The person has a spirit, a soul and a body. It is not permissible to have an open casket, according to Jewish law, so that you don't pretend to yourself that the person is sleeping and will wake up some day. We have no wake, no visitation nor anything of that nature. When the coffin is lowered into the grave, it has to be indeed lowered and the dirt has to be thrown upon it in front of the mourners, before *kaddish* can be recited. Only after the body is in the grave and the dirt has been refilled into the hole in the ground can the person consider himself a mourner and say *kaddish*. He is not technically, according to Jewish law, an *avail,* until that point and then he says the mourner's *kaddish* for the first time, to accept the reality of death.

In the Bible we find stories of life and death. The Bible never glosses over stories of death or murder. The Bible is the bloodiest, sexiest, gutsiest book you every want to read. It has everything in it and it pulls no punches. It tells the truth "just like it is" because it is a book of realism. It doesn't hide harshness, there is no censorship.

Joshua, when he was dying said: "Behold this day I go the way of all the earth." All of us have to go that same way.

It used to be that in a Jewish home young children would study *Hilchot Availut.* A very natural and normal part of growing up was to study the laws of mourning. Every child knew what *shivah, shloshim, yahrzeit, yizkor, kaddish* were, and all these terms were part of Jewish education. It wasn't when somebody was afflicted with a terminal illness in the family that you had to begin studying all these laws. This was taught to every Jewish child. There is a story of a modern Hebrew school in which the teacher was teaching a child to recite mourner's *kaddish.* The father came to see the Hebrew school principal, outraged. "What's the idea of teaching my son the mourner's kaddish. What's going on around here?" The principal assured him: "Don't worry. Until he learns it you will be long gone." But a father in traditional times would refer to his son as "my *kaddish'l*" "my little kaddish." He's the person who will, after I'm gone, recite kaddish. There is no shame, fear, denial, or repression about that. You introduce your son as *"my kaddish'l."* He's the person who is going to say *kaddish* after I'm gone. In a way Judaism has desensitized the whole issue of death. We are not hypersensitive. We can laugh about it, just as we are doing now. We become less sensitive. If we remember studying the laws and witnessing a death in our home and going to a funeral, then death is part of life. If you have hidden it, if you've been protected from it, if your parents have shielded you from the terrible tragedy of death and never exposed you to it, then you are hypersensitive and when you actually come into contact with it, your sensitivity can jar you to the point of creating an emotional illness. That's what Judaism tries to prevent.

We've studied stories of martyrs all through the ages who have given up their life rather than live a life without honor and dignity. These stories help us to respect death as an honorable and inevitable part of all of our lives, some sooner, some later. The story of Rabbi Akiva who was burned at the stake because he refused to give up the study of Torah. There is the lovely story of Rabbi Meir and his wife Bruriah who was a great scholar in her own right. One night when Rabbi Meir was returning from synagogue after the Sabbath evening service, his two young children had died from a sudden illness. Bruriah, before telling him the news, said to him, as he was about to sit down to the Sabbath dinner, "I have a question of law to ask of you." What if somebody came here and lent me a set of beautiful jewels. Then some day He came and said, "I want to take these jewels back, now. They are mine." What would you say? What is Jewish law on that subject? Rabbi Meir said, "you would have to give them back." That's Jewish law, they are only borrowed. Then Bruriah took her husband into the room and showed him the two children. We have here a sense—even in the moment of greatest tragedy—of acceptance of death. Sometimes it is premature, but whenever it happens, life is a gift, and has to be returned whenever the time comes. *We* are not to determine when that time is.

As I indicated earlier, I think we ought to take our children to funerals, we shouldn't shield them from it. Each individual child has his own readiness. I can't say that at age 8 a child should begin attending funerals. But I think somewhere between the age of 8 and 10, depending on the child, he ought to go to the funeral of his aunt, uncle, grandparent, even a friend in the neighborhood. We have to desensitize this whole subject of death, which has been repressed.

Doctors testify that it is very difficult to talk to a patient who has a terminal illness about death if he has never been exposed before - if he has never discussed it, or studied about it, or been to a funeral. It is a most difficult task to discuss death with a dying person, in any case. But at least those who have been to some extent desensitized have the capability of doing so. Otherwise, it is almost impossible. In the old days, I am told, people would prepare their own shrouds, sew them, get them ready, put them on, get ready for their own death. You know it is going to happen. Just as you write a will, buy life insurance, people would buy or make a shroud. I remember in Jerusalem once I went into a synagogue and saw a coffin, nailed up on the wall. I remember being absolutely aghast at seeing this. I asked the rabbi what was the idea. He said, just to prove to everybody, to remind everybody that this is a democratic world, and in the synagogue, we are all equal because this is the end of all of us. Nobody is special, nobody is a big man here. We are all plain, simple ordinary people and that's what's going to be. Every time you walk into that synagogue you are reminded of the necessity of an end to life.

The important thing about the Jewish funeral is its *simplicity* and *democracy*. In the second century Rabban Gamliel said that from now on everyone is going to wear the same garment, a simple, linen shroud. Nobody is allowed to dress anymore as they were then, as they are today in some fancy funeral parlors who violate Jewish law. Even then people would compete with each other to see who had the fancier dress at the funeral. This was established for everyone to be equal. No flowers are permitted because that would be a waste and the best way to honor the dead would be to give tzedaka in the person's memory.

All the above is point number one: that Judaism stresses the reality of death, as a part of life. The second point is that Judaism has a method of gradual return to normalcy through a series of grief rituals. The process of grief is a very slow process and it cannot be rushed. First, when a person suffers a loss in the family, he is technically called an *onen*. From the time of the death until the funeral, a person is not allowed to say the *Sh'ma* or even *ha'motzie* or put on his *tefillin*. Nothing concerns him except the grief which he must begin to face. He is exempt from participating in any ritual. It is not a time for that. Then, from the burial to the 7th day following, that is the *shiva* period, when people come to offer comfort and consolation. *Shiva,* by the way, is a Hebrew word and it means seven. It doesn't mean three, four or five: it means seven. Grief cannot be rushed. It is a very slow process, and it has to be worked out with each individual very carefully. After the *shiva* period there is *sh'loshim,* thirty days of somewhat less mourning, one can go out now, wear his regular clothes and shoes, but nevertheless no entertainment, no partying or that kind of thing. For a parent it is eleven months of saying *kaddish.* For anybody else, such as a spouse, child, sibling, one says *kaddish* and mourns for only thirty days, and that completely terminates the mourning. A very realistic assessment of relationships. Only for a parent it goes on for eleven months. Each year you remember the anniversary of the death through yahrzeit. Four times a year, at holidays, you say *yizkor.* This helps us annually to remember the person. It gives us a specific format for remembering without being morbid, without over-doing it. The important thing here is to express you grief, not to hold it in, or repress it. "Hide not your grief." (From the selection I read from Ben Sira.) When you are visiting a person and trying to help them in the *shiva* period, never say, "O, don't cry, don't feel bad," or to a child "let's behave now," or "don't make mommy sad." Those are the worst kind of things you can do for a person. They must get it out of their system. They must express their grief. If they don't, if they bottle it up, they are planting seeds for emotional illness later on. If you are trying to be helpful to a mourner, don't try to change the subject and keep his mind off his problems. You have to try to keep his mind on it so he can get it out of his system. Don't cheer him up; don't distract him but talk about the deceased, if the mourner feels he is ready. In most cases I find people very willing and very eager to talk about their departed relative.

It's a very difficult thing, I guess, when you are visiting someone to say, tell me about your father, your wife, what kind of person was he or she. You'll find that the mourner is very, very ready to tell you about the person. Often he will laugh about happy and wonderful incidents. It is not always a morbid thing. He can sit there and giggle together about some of the funny things they've experienced in their life time and that's perfectly all right. What's not all right, of course, is when you go to a house of mourning and indulge in all kinds of pleasantries and jokes, try to keep people cheerful, change the atmosphere. There should be a sense of solemnity. There is a place for laughter if it relates to the realities of the situation. It is not all morbid. This was a wonderful person. He or she lived a long and good life. Let's be happy about that.

There is a place for happiness but not of telling jokes and of gossiping, of long conversations, of talking to your neighbor. Many people don't really see the mourner when they visit. They walk in, shake hands and talk to all their friends and use it for a social hour. That's wrong. One should stay for 5 or 10 minutes. Once you have finished talking to the mourner, just turn around, put your coat on and go home and let other people get to the mourner. A crowded house, a noisy house is not of help and neither is the obligation for them to serve all kinds of meals and food to people. A very simple outlay is sufficient, certainly not to be catered as it is in many large cities.

One of the things we have to keep in mind with people who have suffered a loss is that inevitably a mourner will feel guilty about something in their relationship with the deceased. They might feel they didn't do enough for the dead while they lived. Perhaps they feel if they had been in a better hospital, obtained better medical care or had been visited more often; if you were out to make that last visit and you don't get there in time—countless opportunities for people to feel guilty. After all, the truth is that we never do enough for other people, for anybody, for ourselves. It's not possible. So there is this ready ground for guilty feelings. It's natural. You may have had an argument with the person, you may have spoken some cruel words, recently or a long time ago, which will crop up into your mind, make you feel terrible; you may even have wished them dead, possibly, when you got into an argument. "Gee, I wish this person would just drop dead and get out of my life." If a week or a month later it happens, imagine how you feel. This is a reality. The mourner has to work these things through in his mind and say to himself, I didn't have a perfect relationship with this individual; nobody has a perfect relationship with anybody. She was a good mother to me; we had our fights, our disagreements, I got her angry, I may have said things I didn't mean but that's all right we can forgive ourselves for those things because nobody is perfect. But it takes a while to be able to forgive. The immediate reaction is to feel, "Oh, my goodness, I had a part in this death."

One of the things that helps a person in working through the feeling of guilt is the concrete expression of doing something positive for the deceased by creating a memorial, by having people give *tzedaka,* by speaking nicely, hearing a nice eulogy—all these things help to overcome that sense of guilt that we inevitably feel. A very positive concrete action is to go to synagogue and to say the mourner's *kaddish.* These are the grief rituals of Judaism, that help us to overcome our sense of helplessness, loneliness, alienation and guilt for the things we didn't do. I think, by the way, that women should say *kaddish*. Traditionally it is only the obligation of the men but there is no reason in the world why a woman shouldn't say *kaddish*. Every time I go to a *shiva* home as soon as I say "services begin on page 120," all the women scurry into the kitchen and begin to drink a cup of coffee. Only the men remain for services. That's ridiculous and shouldn't be. All the women who are there should remain for the service and the women who are mourners should say *kaddish*. That goes for the cemetary as well as for the home services and for the period of time, month or year, (depending on the relative) afterward.

Henrietta Szold wrote a very beautiful letter in September 1916: "It's impossible for me to find words in which to tell you how deeply I was touched by your offer to act as a kaddish-sayer for my dear mother. I cannot thank you. It is something that goes beyond thanks. It's beautiful. I shall never forget it. You will wonder then why I cannot accept your offer. Perhaps it would be best if I not try to explain to you in writing but wait until I see you. I know well and appreciate what you say about the Jewish custom. Jewish custom is sacred to me. Yet I cannot ask you to say kaddish after my mother. Kaddish means to me that the survivor publicly and markedly manifests his wish and intention to assume his relation to the Jewish community which his parent had so that the chain of tradition remains unbroken from generation to generation each adding its own link. You can only do that for the generations of your family. I must do that for the generations of my family. I believe that the elimination of women from such duties was never intended by our law. Women were free from the positive duties which they could not perform but not when they could. It was never intended if they could perform them that the performance of them should not be considered as valuable and valid as when the male sex performed them. Of the kaddish I feel sure that this is particularly true. My mother had eight daughters and no sons. Yet never did I hear a word of regret pass the lips of either my mother or my father that not one of us was a son. When my father died, my mother did not permit others to take her daughters', places in saying the kaddish. So I am sure I am acting in her spirit when I decline your offer." Thus, Henrietta Szold, a great Jewish lady with a great Jewish message.

One of the ways to overcome our sense of loss and grief is to find a new object for our love and affection. That doesn't mean that you didn't love your husband, your parent, your child, whoever the person is, but we all have to express our affection. We all need to love people. When one object of affection is removed from our lives it should be replaced. Find a charity. If the person died of a disease perhaps it would be a good idea to work for an organization fighting that disease. If it is a child that died, then work for a children's organization or find another friend, or whatever it is, find an outlet for your affection.

I think it is a bad idea to visit the mourner in the funeral home. They sit up either in the front row, or in the little side room and streams of people file through. I think they should be left alone. I think we ought to leave the mourner with his grief. *Pirke Avot,* 2000 years ago, said, "Do not comfort your fellow while his dead lies before him." That's not a time for comforting. That's a time to be left alone with your own grief. There is a time and a place for everything.

The unveiling is a good way to express our completion of the year of grief so that it gets us one more step closer to normalcy. Now the year is over, we are ready to get back to our normal way of life. I don't think, however, that unveilings should be the kind they are today. Unveiling is not a Jewish custom, has no tradition in Judaism. Putting up a marker is

proper in Jewish law but having an unveiling of the stone is
not. I suggest that people with their immediate family pay a
visit to the grave, without a rabbi or a cantor, by themselves.
We have a few prayers to give out to say; don't make a big
party of it or a second funeral and invite people back for food,
or send out invitations as some people do. Just five or six of
you, the immediate family, go visit the grave when the year is
up, take the veil off the marker, say the *Ayl Molei Rachamim,*
and the twenty-third Psalm. That's all that need be done.
After the first year, we are back to life. The third point I want
to make is that the end of one's life should have dignity and
peace.

Should a dying patient be told of his illness? Most of the
authorities that I have read say that the dying person finds out
sooner or later anyway. Better to be told earlier when you can
determine the context to tell the person rather than having
him find out when he can read it in your face, and can see that
the nurses are a little bit reluctant to go into the room, or
hurry out very quickly. Very few people come in to see them
anymore. They begin to feel isolated. Few people talk to them
any more, they are frightened, not of this person's dying but of
their own death. We are so afraid of our own death that we
can't face somebody else's dying, bringing it too close to
home. Repression and denial again. In the case of most
people, depending on their make-up, they should be told in a
proper, sensitive way, so that they can prepare themselves, do
the things that they need to do before their death. If the
person has had the proper preparation for it then ultimately
he will be ready for it.

When a person views the death of another individual or is
told of his own terminal illness, there will be the immediate
reaction of denial. It can't be—a mistaken diagnosis, we have
to check with another doctor. It's just impossible. After that
initial reaction they begin to be angry. These are stages which

the psychologists have observed in dying people. Beginning to be angry, they ask, "Why me? I am a young person, what have I done to deserve this?" They try to postpone in various ways the thought of death, because nobody can really live with the thought of his own death. We try to think of ways to postpone it which is natural and healthy.

Then there is the stage of depression—real grief and sadness and isolation. Finally, for most people, a stage of acceptance when they realize what is happening, they are ready and willing (even though nobody is ever happy or satisfied with his own death but at least accepting it). Nevertheless, we always maintain hope. The dying person never thinks it is going to be today. He hopes that the ultimate end will be postponed as long as possible, and it can very well be postponed. There are all kinds of new medications coming out every day, new methods, new technology. If a person gives up hope, if they say it will be all over in a couple of days, then it really might happen in a couple of days. You have to have some kind of hope, that whatever time is left is going to be as good, as happy a period of their life as it can be. I've seen many people very bravely live through a wonderful end of their lives in that way. The French scholar, Montaigne, said, "Death is just a moment when dying ends." Nobody knows how long it will be until we die. We are all dying because ultimately we will die. Each day we get older, our body degenerates and deteriorates. Death is that one second, that one moment when dying ends.

A student nurse was once told about her imminent death. She wrote this: "I am a student nurse. I am dying. I write this to you who are, and will become, nurses in the hope that by my sharing my feelings with you, you may someday be better able to help those who share my experience.

"I'm out of the hospital now, perhaps for a month, for six months, perhaps for a year . . . but no one likes to talk about such things. In fact, no one likes to talk about much at all. Nursing must be advancing, but I wish it would hurry. We're taught not to be overly cheery now, to omit the "Everything's fine" routine, and we have done it pretty well. But now one is left in a lonely silent void. With the protective "fine, fine" gone, the staff is left with only their own vulnerability and fear. The dying patient is not yet seen as a person and thus cannot be communicated with as such. He is a symbol of what every human fears and what we each know, at least academically, that we too must someday face. What did they say in psychiatric nursing about meeting pathology with pathology to the detriment of both patient and nurse? And there was a lot about knowing one's own feelings before you could help another with his. How true.

"But for me, fear is today and dying is now. You slip in and out of my room, give me medications and check my blood pressure. Is it because I am a student nurse, myself, or just a human being, that I sense your fright? And your fear enhances mine. Why are you afraid? I am the one who is dying!

"I know, you feel insecure, don't know what to say, don't know what to do. But please believe me, if you care, you can't go wrong. Just admit that you care. That is really for what we search. We may ask for why's and wherefores, but we don't really expect answers. Don't run away . . . wait . . . all I want to know is that there will be someone to hold my hand when I need it. I am afraid. Death may get to be a routine to you, but it is new to me. You may not see me as unique, but I've never died before. To me, once is pretty unique!

"You whisper about my youth, but when one is dying, is he really so young anymore? I have lots I wish we could talk about. It really would not take much more of your time because you are in here quite a bit anyway.

"If only we could be honest, both admit of our fears, touch one another. If you really care, would you lose so much of your valuable professionalism if you even cried with me? Just person to person? Then, it might not be so hard to die . . . in a hospital . . . with friends close by."

A word about euthanasia. Again, it is a very complex subject which deserves a whole lecture of itself but I personally believe that all the artificial medical life support systems which are pumped into a patient who is more or less dead anyway is unrealistic, unfair. I think there is good precedent for that in Jewish law when people were told in the Talmud, "Don't pray for this person." They believed that prayer had the same effectiveness that we believe medicine does. Really what they were saying was, "Don't prolong this individual's life." When the time of death comes, let the person slip into death. Particularly if the person has been reduced to a vegetable and there is no hope any more at all. They have a medical term now that they call "brain death." This describes an irreversible coma, when a person's mind is gone. After oxygen has been cut off from the mind for a sufficient period of time so that his capacity has been erased. Unresponsiveness non-receptivity, no reflex action—all this is "brain death." When a person has no mind, tracheotomies and oxygen and injections and all the things we do for them are unnecessary and are wrong. The choice ought to be left to the individual. I am told that Sigmund Freud asked a close physician friend when he was close to death to just give him a few shots of morphine and end it all.

In many senses, I think medicine by its great strides in prolonging life has dehumanized life, dehumanized the human being. It is very difficult to determine when that point is, of course, and I don't think that a person should be directly put to death. That is a different point altogether. But I think that what is called "indirect euthanasia," the approach of not sustaining life artificially, is something that Jewish law would recommend.

In conclusion I think if a person has had a good life, he will have a good death, whenever it comes—at age twenty, fifty, or ninety. If you live a good life, you will have a good death. Life is not measured in quantity. Some people live in twenty-five years more than others live in seventy-five years. The Rabbis say, repent one day before your death. None of us knows when he is going to die. That means expect it tomorrow. While we are alive, however, take each day one at a time, whether we have a year to live or 60 years to live. Just take each day and make the best of it. Then we will be ready when death comes.

In the morning service, there is a beautiful prayer recited by pious Jews, *Elohai neshama,* which expresses the thought that when we wake up in the morning it is like being restored to life after being in a state of something similar to death. We are revived. The prayer says, "O, my God, the soul Thou has given to me is pure. Thou didst create it, Thou didst form it, Thou didst breathe it into me. Thou preservest it within me. Thou wilt take it from me. But will restore it unto me hereafter. So long as the soul is within me, I will give thanks unto Thee. Lord my God, God of my fathers, Sovereign of all work, Lord of all souls. Blessed art Thou, O Lord, who restorest souls unto dead."

Finally, I want to read a lovely prayer which was written by one of my late teachers at the Jewish Theological Seminary. A beautiful poem, by Hillel Bavli, which is included in the new High Holy Day *Mahzor,* called "Zot Tefilati," "This is my Prayer."

Let me not swerve from my life's path,
Let not my spirit wither and shrivel
In its thirst for You
And lose the dew
With which You sprinkled it
When I was young.

May my heart be open
To every broken soul,
To orphaned life,
To every stumbler
Wandering unknown
And groping in the shadow.

Bless my eyes, purify me to see
Man's beauty rise in the world.

Deepen and broaden my senses
To absorb a fresh
Green, flowering world.
To take from it the secret
Of blossoming in silence.

Grant strength to yield fine fruits,
Quintessence of my life,
Steeped in my very being,
Without expectation of reward.

And when my time comes—
Let me slip into the night
Demanding nothing, God, of man,
Or of You.

Books Containing Activities and Structured Experiences for Human Relations Training in Classroom and Other Groups

Compiled by Dov Peretz Elkins
September 1975

Teaching Is...by Merrill Harmin and Tom Gregory, Chicago: Science Research Assoc., Inc. 1974

Born To Win by Muriel James and Dorothy Jongeward, Reading, Mass.: Addison-Wesley Pub. Co., 1971

Self-Awareness Through Group Dynamics by Richard Reichert, Dayton, Ohio: Pflaum Pub., 1970

Meeting Yourself Halfway by Sidney B. Simon, Inles, Ill.: Argus Communications, 1974

A Guide To Developing Your Potential by Herbert A. Otto, No. Hollywood, Cal.: Wilshire Book Co., 1967

Teaching Human Beings - 101 Subversive Articles for the Classroom by Jeffrey Schrank, Boston, Mass.: Beacon Press, 1972

Growing Up Alive by Tim Timmerman, Mandala. P.O. Box 796, Amherst, Mass. 01002

Circlebook - A Leader Handbook for Conducting Circletime, Jim Ballard, Mandala, P.O. Box 796, Amherst, Mass. 01002

Human Communication Handbook - Simulations and Games by Brent D. Ruben and Richard W. Budd, Rochelle Park, N.J.: Hayden Book Co., Inc. 1975

Values in Sexuality - A New Approach to Sex Education by Eleanor S. Morrison and Mila Underhill Price. N.Y.: Hart, 1974

Awareness: Exploring, Experimenting, Experiencing by John O. Stevens, Moab, Utah: Real People Press, 1971

Developing Human Potential - Structured Experiences in Awareness, Potency, and Relatedness by Therese Livingston-Smith, Harleysville, Pa.: Institute for Personal Effectiveness, 1975

Clarifying Value Through Subject Matter: Applications for the classroom by Merrill Harmin, Howard Kirschenbaum, Sidney B. Simon, Minneapolis, Minn.: Winston, Press, Inc., 1973

Values Clarification: A Handbook Of Practical Strategies For Teachers and Students by Sidney B. Simon, Leland W. Howe, Howard Kirschenbaum, N.Y. : Hart Publishing Co., 1972

More Values Clarification - Strategies for the Classroom by Sidney B. Simon and Jay Clark, San Diego: Pennant Press, 1975

Personalizing Education: Values Clarification and Beyond - Over One Hundred Strategies, Plus Work Sheets by Leland W. Howe and Mary Martha Howe, N.Y.: Hart Publishing Co., 1975

Reaching Out - Interpersonal Effectiveness and Self-Actualization by David W. Johnson, Englewood Cliffs, N.J.: Prentice-Hall, 1972

Peer Program For Youth - A Group Interaction Plan by Ardyth Hebeisen, Minneapolis, Minn.: Augsburg Publishing House, 1973

Handbooks of Structured Experiences by J. William Pfeiffer and John E. Jones, 5 Volumes, LaJolla, Cal.: University Associates, 1971-5

The 1972, 1973, 1974, and 1975 Annual Handbooks For Group Facilitators by J. William Pfeiffer and John E. Jones, LaJolla, Calif.: University Associates, 1972-75

Reference Guide to Handbooks and Annuals by J. William Pfeiffer and John E. Jones, LaJolla, Calif.: University Associates, 1975

X-Ed—Experiential Education by John and Lela Hendrix, Nashville, Tenn.: Abingdon, 1975

A Humanistic Psychology of Education: Making the School Everybody's House by Richard A. Schmuck and Patricia A. Schmuck. Palo Alto, Cal.: Mayfield Publishing Co., 1974

One Hundred Ways to Enhance Self-Concept in the Classroom by Jack Canfield and Harold Wells, Englewood Cliffs, N.J.: Prentice-Hall, 1975

Value Clarification - As Learning Process - A Handbook for Christian Educators by Brian P. Hall and Maury Smith, Paramus, N.J.: Paulist Press, 1973

Value Clarification in the Classroom: A Primer by J. Doyle Casteel and Robert J. Stahl, Pacific Palisades, Cal.: Goodyear Publishing Co., 1975

The Guide to Simulations/Games For Education and Training by David W. Zuckerman and Robert E. Horn, Lexington, Mass.: Information Resources, Inc., 1973

Learning Discussion Skills Through Games by Gene Stanford and Barbara Dodds, Stanford, N.Y.: Citation Press, 1969

Games For Growth—Educational Games in the Classroom by Alice Kaplan Gordon, Chicago: Science Research Assoc., 1972

Human Values in the Classroom—A Handbook for Teachers by Robert C. Hawley and Isabel L. Hawley, N.Y.: Hart Pub. Co., 1975

Winning With People—Group Exercises and Transactional Analysis, by Muriel James and Dorothy Jongeward.

Twenty Exercises for the Classroom. NTL Learning Resources Corp. 1972

Personal Growth Thru Groups: A Collection of Methods by Martin I. Seldman and David Hermes, The "We Care Foundation," 121 Broadway, San Diego, Calif. 1975

Group Methods to Actualize Human Potential—A Handbook by Herbert Otto, Beverly Hills, Cal.: The Holistic Press, 1973

Nine New Group Methods To Actualize Human Potential: A Handbook by Herbert Otto, Beverly Hills, Cal.: The Holistic Press, 1973

Threads—Techniques for Human Relations Programs for Children by Avis Reid, The Open Door, 205 W. 16th Street, Glencoe, Minn. 55336, $6.50.

A Handbook for Personal Growth Activities for Classroom Use by Robert C. Hawley and Isabel L. Hawley, Education Research Associates, Box 767, Amherst, Mass. 01002, 1972, $5.

Developing Human Potential - A Handbook of Activities for Personal and Social Growth by Robert C. Hawley and Isabel L. Hawley, Educational Research Associates, Box 767, Amherst, Mass., 01002, 1975. $4.95.

Selected Readings in Humanistic Psychology

George Bach
The Intimate Enemy
Creative Aggression

Eric Berne
Games People Play

John H. Brennecke and Robert G. Amick
The Struggle for Significance
Significance: The Struggle We Share

James F.T. Bugental
The Search for Authenticity
Challenges of Humanistic Psychology

Charlotte Buhler and Melanie Allen
Introduction to Humanistic Psychology

Dov Peretz Elkins
Glad to Be Me: Building Self-Esteem in Yourself and Others

Viktor Frankl
Man's Search for Meaning

Erich Fromm
The Art of Loving

John V. Gilmore
The Productive Personality

Haim Ginott
Between Parent and Child
Between Parent and Teenager
Between Teacher and Student

Frank G. Goble
  The Third Force
Thomas Gordon
  Parent Effectiveness Training
  Teacher Effectiveness Training
Thomas C. Greening
  Existential Humanistic Psychology
Jerry Greenwald
  How To Be the Person You Were Meant To Be
Thomas Harris
  I'm OK You're OK
Sidney Jourard
  Healthy Personality
  The Transparent Self
Gerald and Elisabeth Jud
  Training in the Art of Loving
John Mann
  Learning to Be
Abraham Maslow
  Motivation and Personality
  Toward a Psychology of Being
  Religions, Values and Peak Experiences
  The Farther Reaches of Human Nature
Rollo May
  Existence
  Love and Will
  Power and Innocence
Clark Moustakas
  Individual and Encounter
  Personal Growth
  Finding Yourself, Finding Others
  The Authentic Teacher
George and Nena O'Neil
  Shifting Gears
  Open Marriage

Herbert Otto
Developing Your Potential
More Joy in Your Marriage
Ways of Growth

Fritz Perls
Gestalt Therapy Verbatim
In and Out the Garbage Pail

Severin Peterson
A Catalog of the Ways People Grow

Carl Rogers
On Becoming a Person
Freedom to Learn
Person to Person
Becoming Partners

Virginia Satir
Peoplemaking

William Schutz
Joy
Here Comes Everybody

Frank T. Severin
Discovering Man in Psychology - A Humanistic Approach

Everett Shostrom
Man the Manipulator
Freedom to Be

Sidney Simon (et al)
Values and Teaching
Values Clarification
Readings in Values Clarification

Bibliography

Allport, Gordon W. *The Individual and His Religion.* New York: The Macmillan Company, 1960.

Birnbaum, Philip. *A Book of Jewish Concepts.* New York: Hebrew Publishing Company, 1964.

Bolton, Robert. *A Reinventive Faith.* Cazenovia, New York: Center on the Ridge, no date.

Buber, Martin. *Hasisdism and Modern Man.* New York: Harper, 1958.

Buber, Martin. *Tales of the Hasidism.* New York: Schocken, 1947 and 1948.

Clinebell, Howard J., Jr. *The Mental Health Ministry of the Local Church.* Nashville, Tenn.: Abingdon, 1972.

Coleman, Lyman. *Serendipity Frog Kissin' Workshops.* Scottdale, Pa.: Serendipity House, 1974.

Egan, Gerard. *The Skilled Helper.* Monterey, California: Brooks/Cole, 1974.

Fromm, Erich. *Psychoanalysis and Religion.* New Haven, Conn.: Yale University Press, 1950.

Fromm, Erich. *The Art of Living.* New York: Harper, 1958.

Glustrom, Simon. *The Language of Judaism.* New York: Ktav, 1974.

Goble, Frank G. *The Third Force: The Psychology of Abraham Maslow.* New York: Pocket Books, 1971.

Good, Paul, editor. *The Individual.* New York: Time-Life Books, 1974.

Jourard, Sidney M. *Healthy Personality, An Approach From the Viewpoint of Humanistic Psychology.* New York: Macmillan, 1974.

Kadushin, Max. *Worship and Ethics: A Study in Rabbinic Judaism.* Northeastern University Press, 1963.

Lamm, Norman. *The Royal Reach.* New York: Phillip Feldheim, 1970.

Link, Mark. *In the Stillness Is the Dancing.* Niles, Illinois: Argus Communications, 1972.

Maltz, Maxwell. *Psycho-Cybernetics and Self-Fulfillment.* New York: Bantam Books, 1973.

Maslow, Abraham H. "Neurosis as a Failure of Personal Growth," from *Humanitas,* 1973, pages 153-169.

Meininger, Jut. *Success Through Transactional Analysis.* New York: New American Library, 1974.

Moore, Donald J. Martin Buber: *Prophet of Religious Secularism.* Philadelphia: Jewish Publication Society, 1974.

Moustakas, Clark. *Individuality and Encounter.* Cambridge, Mass.: Howard A. Doyle Publishing Company, 1968.

Perls, Fritz. *Ego, Hunter, and Aggression.* New York: Random House, 1969.

Ram Dass. *The Only Dance There Is.* Garden City, L.I., New York: Anchor Press/Doubleday, 1974.

Shepard, Martin. *Fritz: An Intimate Portrait of Fritz Perls and Gestalt Therapy.* New York: Saturday Review Press, 1975.

Siegel, Richard, and others, editors. *The Jewish Catalog.* Philadelphia: Jewish Publication Society, 1974.

Stein, Joseph. *Effective Personality; A Humanistic Approach.* Belmont, California: Brooks/Cole, 1972.

Index